Desktop Hosting:

A Developer's Guide to Unattended Communications

Desktop Hosting:

A Developer's Guide to Unattended Communications

Bill James

Wiley Publishing, Inc.

Publisher: Robert Ipsen
Editor: Ben Ryan
Developmental Editor: Kathryn A. Malm
Managing Editor: Angela Smith
New Media Editor: Brian Snapp
Text Composition: John Wiley Composition Services

This book is printed on acid-free paper. ♾

Published by Wiley Publishing, Inc., New York

Published simultaneously in Canada.

For general information on our other products and services please contact our Customer Care Department within the United States at (800) 762-2974, outside the United States at (317) 572-3993 or fax (317) 572-4002.

Wiley also publishes its books in a variety of electronic formats. Some content that appears in print may not be available in electronic books.

Library of Congress Cataloging-in-Publication Data:

James, Bill.
Desktop hosting : a developer's guide to unattended communications /
Bill James.
p. cm.
Includes index.
ISBN 0-471-20767-5 (PAPER/CD-ROM : alk. paper)
1. Web servers. 2. Microcomputers. 3. Web site development. I.
Title.
TK5105.888 .J35 2002
004.67'8—dc21

2002007077

Printed in the United States of America.

10 9 8 7 6 5 4 3 2 1

CONTENTS

ACKNOWLEDGMENTS

This book is a team effort of many people in many areas. Specifically, I would like to thank:

Customers of JITCorp who have provided so much insight into what is needed in the market.

Team at JITCorp of Leanna Peterson, Jody Reinhardt, Mike Cassano, Brian Widel, Chris James, Lissa Read, Ronnie Miller, Tom Harrington, Travis James and others who contributed so much for so long to build and document our "Empire in a Thimble."

Christian Quest of ITK for the IP language which so powerfully supported our development.

Ben Ryan and Angela Smith at Wiley for the publishing support.

INTRODUCTION

Communications is the aspect of leadership that unites the diverse interests of vendors, employees, shareholders, and customers in the effort to profit from their relationship with your company. It clarifies and brands the value of a relationship with your company. Communicating better provides a competitive advantage. Striving for this advantage has driven improvements to put the point-of-communications at the point-of-action:

Attended communications exploded, with many people carrying cell phones.

Print communications, with desktop publishing, allowed everyone to create rich documents on the desktop.

Unattended communications have progressed from telegram, to telex, to fax, to email. But each of these efforts requires the customer to invest labor to ask the question, and you must invest labor to receive the message, interpret it, and answer it. Every action is a potential point of failure.

The objective of this book is to help you change your company's unattended communications from the impersonal "Leave a message" to a personal, published response: "Here is your answer." Desktop Hosting puts the point of communication at the point of action for unattended communications.

Desktop Hosting changes unattended communications from message-based to publish-based. It automates interactions with contacts based on the relationship with the contact and the desired results. Examples are:

- My daughter sees if I will make it to her game tonight.
- My mom sees the latest movies/pictures of my daughter's game.
- My customers see their order status, recent shipments, account balance, new products I think they should consider, service requests, and so forth.
- My vendors see items I need quoted, their account status, and so forth.

Your local computer is an interactive relationship server; transaction manager and file server, making up-to-the-second information available to the appropriate person. As the requester or information changes, your desktop machine adjusts to meet requests with "Here is your answer."

The Web has created a dramatic change in communications. Unfortunately, most implementations that are affordable focus on centralized concepts. As in the mainframe computing heyday, hosting companies say, in effect, "Web technology is too hard and costly for you to manage. We will serve for you. Host with us." These Web sites are generally marketing, not sales, tools. They display information. They do not fundamentally change the static response of "Leave a message." They do not make the Web a dynamic selling tool. Desktop Hosting will change static marketing Web sites to dynamic sales tools.

Who This Book Is For

This book is designed to assist you in evaluating the consequences of implementing dynamic, unattended communications and making the change to Desktop Hosting. It organizes the concepts, benefits, and how-to instructions into separate sections so that readers with various needs and skills can manage, access and implement a Desktop Hosting solution. There are three parts to this book: Part One, "What is Desktop Hosting," Chapters 1 through 4, covers concepts and should be read by business leaders, students, and developers who want to understand the concepts and budgeting requirements of Desktop Hosting.

Skills required: No special skills are required for this section, although a basic familiarity with the Web, with concepts of clients and server computers, and the nature of databases is assumed.

Part Two, "How Desktop Hosting Works," Chapters 5 through 7, outlines the benefits of Desktop Hosting to various groups within a company and how to train them. Department leaders should read the appropriate chapter(s).

Skills required: No special skills are required for this section, and if you are not already comfortable with HTML and other aspects of Web development, you will start getting your feet wet here. The case studies presented in Chapter 7 are most effective when you work through the accompanying exercises.

Part Three, "Getting Started with the Programs," Chapter 8, introduces WebClerk software that is provided free with this book so you can implement Desktop Hosting solutions at a very low cost. Additional documentation is on the CD which accompanies this book.

What's on the CD-ROM

Included on the CD-ROM are full-featured versions of two integrated applications (single-user compilations of CommerceExpert and WebClerk, a retail value of $849). These applications allow you to experiment and implement your Desktop Hosting solution without additional software cost. To use this program you must register your copy at www.webclerk.com. There is additional help and information at www.WebClerk.com and www.DesktopHosting.com.

WebClerk and CommerceExpert comprise a business system with integrated intranet and extranet capabilities. WebClerk is a database-driven Web server and prefabricated Web site that implements catalogs, order entry, service, libraries, and secure credit card transactions. CommerceExpert is an Enterprise Sales and Operations (ESO) program designed to make your company sales-driven. Reference guides and interactive lessons are provided with the CD.

Skills required: Keep your approach simple. The program is comprehensive, which can equate to complex. It is a business system, database, Web server, and prefabricated Web site. Keep in mind that you do not have to grasp all the details at once and that you can use the standard tools provided to gain experience with the concepts. Once the concepts are under control, you can be as creative as you wish.

The basic implementation does not require any special skills. Modifying the Web site to meet individual graphical and functional variations requires an understanding of Web page design. Importing your products and customers to the program requires data manipulation and database understanding. But if you already have a Web site, you or someone in your company probably already has most of these skills. The look and feel of existing Web sites can be adapted to WebClerk.

Summary

The objective of this book is to create a Desktop Hosting market by defining its concepts and providing tools to actually implement solutions. This is a handbook; part of it is about the concepts and part of it supports actually achieving the objectives of Desktop Hosting.

The tools discussed have been created by my company and are provided to assist you in changing concepts into experience. Tools from other companies will be available as time progresses. It is beyond the scope of this book to provide a list of these tools. To support this industry we have created an industry-neutral site at www.DesktopHosting.com. This interactive site is for reviewing tools and techniques for this industry. Information seekers and competitors are welcome to submit information and participate. I hope that this book helps you implement technologies that add value to your communications, drive down your costs and strengthen the relationships between you and your customers. I hope it is profitable.

PART ONE

Why Desktop Hosting?

CHAPTER 1

Put the Point of Communications at the Point of Action

The Web is perhaps the most dramatic change in communication since voice over wire. The prefix e has been applied to every word that is not fast enough to escape. There is no doubt that the Web is potent. But the dot.com meltdown underscores that applying this technology must still be done within the framework of achieving the fundamental business objective of profitability.

Profitability, adding more value than the cost to compete—not technology—should be a primary objective of every for-profit business. Profit is achieved by the way we lead our companies, communicate value, and coordinate activities to produce it while controlling costs. Communications is a central aspect of leadership; it is not a separate activity.

Changing technological capabilities must be integrated into how leaders communicate with customers, vendors, and allies. Communications must not be separated as an information technology function. What works in business is reinforcing existing relationships with communication advances. Efforts to attack existing supply chains by companies such as Wine.com, WebVan.com, Amazon.com, and Pets.com will not unleash the true profitability promise of the Web. This will be realized as existing supply chain companies integrate their intranets and extranets with their trading partners into a comprehensive supply chain suite.

Unfortunately, many suppliers of technology are trying to sell products or services that force their customers to treat this changing technology separately from their current ability to buy, sell, and deliver service. By separating communications from the ability to sell and service, e-solutions are actually a disservice to the user of the technology. They remove the point of communications from the point of action. They put technology barriers between customers and those they know and trust.

Technology is always changing. These changes must be adapted to the ways we are successfully relating to and working with trading partners. What works is doing business with those we know and trust. What works is communicating and coordinating, uniting and leading the diffuse interests of customers, vendors, allies, and shareholders in an arrangement where more value is added than consumed.

Communications is how we keep our relationships fresh. It is how we align the efforts of our people, suppliers, and allies. It is an integral aspect of leadership and must be an integral part of every aspect of your business planning and execution. It is a means by which you apply your leadership to achieve your company's objectives. Technology should reinforce existing trusted relationships, not attack them.

This book is a communication. You are my customer. To achieve a profitable state in our relationship we need to share a common objective of producing more value than the cost of our efforts. The objective of this handbook is to increase your profitable sales within your existing markets by more than the cost of implementing Desktop Hosting, and to do so within six months. To achieve this objective, we will cover the following elements:

Desktop Hosting. Define and illustrate Desktop Hosting, explain how it effectively integrates the power and advantages of the Web with a company's efforts to increase profitable sales and better serve existing customers.

Assumptions. Define business assumptions and principles on which the book is based so that you can interpret how to adjust concepts to your organization.

Design Basics. Provide design concepts for Desktop Hosting. Why did the dot.com gold rush to the Internet fail? How does an average business compete with the millions that are spent by companies like Amazon.com?

Planning. Provide a planning mechanism so that your company can act quickly to secure a competitive advantage as changes occur.

Examples. Provide case studies of real-world situations that show how some of the complexities in real business can be technologically supported.

Execution. Provide tools and lessons for applying these concepts. Included in this book are the software programs and example data sets to implement the concepts presented. The learning exercises give you hands-on experience integrating your physical business with the Web's capability to communicate with your customers, vendors, and allies and to service their needs.

What Are Desktop Hosting and Unattended Communications?

Desktop Hosting is data-driven, relationship-aware, dynamic, published-based, unattended communications. It will change the competitive landscape because better communications reinforce current business relationships and provide an avenue for expanding relationships to new partners. Communication is the means by which you assure your customers understand the value you provide. Value paid for less the cost to compete is profit. There is always a demand for sales and profits; therefore, there is always a demand for better communications to bind our business relationships. Because sales often depend on a personal relationship between the buyer and seller, there is a constant demand to put the point of communication at the point of action, to be available to your trading partners with the right answer, at the right time. You can see this demand for better communications in attended communications by looking for the nearest cell phone.

NOTE

Desktop Hosting is data-driven, relationship-aware, dynamic, published-based, unattended communications.

Unattended communications—how we connect when we cannot pick up the phone—is far behind advances in attended communications. Unattended communications has progressed from mail to telegraph to telex to fax to email and voice mail. But these advances are all message-based. The requester invests labor to ask a question and receives a static "Please leave a message" response. This is about to change.

Desktop Hosting will change unattended communications *from message-based to published-based*, from a universally unresponsive "Leave a message" to a dynamic, relationship-aware "Here's your answer." It changes e-commerce from a separate, remote task to an integrated, multifaceted, relationship-supporting communication and commerce system. To handle the nuances that give your sales and operations departments competitive edge, Desktop Hosting will be served from the desktops within your company.

This shift in unattended communications is similar to other technology changes. Mainframe computing gave way to desktops, laptops, and palms. Desktop publishing changed print communications from a remote service to a personal ability to create and distribute print and multimedia communications. Desktop Hosting allows the creation of many communications that are finely tuned to those receiving them.

Your staff considers their desktops to be the fulcrum, the pivot points where detailed knowledge and understanding of each relationship is shared with your trading partners. It is the place you put phones for attended communications. Making the Web interactive at this critical point leverages your ability to build and sustain relationships.

How many transactions occur every day to make a business competitive? How many different conversations occur between buyers and vendors, shippers and carriers, service and customers, sales and customers? To support these critical transactions and conversations, businesses put phones on everyone's desktop. Having a monolithic e-commerce Web site is like having a switchboard handle all these conversations and is unlikely to adapt to the subtleties that bind you to your trading partners. Desktop Hosting—by integrating data, relationships and communications at the point of action—will change this and the competitive landscape.

When you look around at the computers in your company, you often see little memory triggers: small piles of paper notes, Post-It notes stuck on the sides of computer monitors, lists on whiteboards, and other reminders. These typically indicate at least one transaction that your business and communication systems have had to work around.

> *The devil is in the details.*
>
> Unknown

Leanna Peterson (my Chief of Staff) and Craig Johnson (Chairman of Venture Law) each came up with analogies when they considered Desktop Hosting. Craig looked at Desktop Hosting as it is applied by Wine Operations, Inc., and noted:

> *All the most valuable information about products, preferences, price, delivery, etc., is located at the fringes of a customer/manufacturer/distributor communications network, and attempts to centralize and manage the relevant details in a single database are overwhelmed by the magnitude of the task and the upkeep. It's the same reason managed economies are less efficient than market-based ones. Bill James' distributed approach to communications tools—giving tools to the people who must act—puts the ability to manage information where it is most useful and beneficial to customer relationships.*

Leanna considered the concepts from distributed and organizational viewpoints in a paper for her master's degree:

> *Desktop Hosting enables a bottoms-up concept whereby computing power, data hosting, and business logic are distributed among multitudes of small desktops that transmit data to each other upon demand. An analogy is: Drive the management of the data to the tip of the tree branch, instead of consolidating data in the center trunk.*
>
> *An example that has already taken the world by storm is Napster, which turned participating desktops into [music] file transfer servers. This is the same concept, only the participating desktops are trading operational data. Push a button to check on all pending orders, similar to a central email service that consolidates messages from a variety of other email servers.*

This approach is the opposite of many centralized operational applications, which can be cumbersome, and difficult to integrate with a Web interface. The whole Desktop Hosting concept is nimble and cheap, and—if used within an organization—establishes a series of contracts among organizational entities that permit each entity to behave in a customer-oriented fashion.

Desktop Hosting moves the leaves back to the end of the branches. The rush to implement Web communications made the assumption that every transaction is equal, that all needed to be centrally controlled and centrally managed. But like leaves and sunshine, many transactions can only occur when properly distributed.

Distributing the power to communicate to every branch of your organization is a fundamental precept of our approach. To be competitive, your company needs the judgment of many of your people. Running your business takes too much expertise to be centrally controlled; it is more effective to keep the leaves at the end of the branches. Like leaves on a tree, spread your communications capabilities to interact with the sunshine that sustains your company, the relationships with customers.

Table 1.1 describes examples of the change between message- and published-based unattended communications. Figures 1.1 and 1.2 show the buyer/seller interactions that occur during these communications.

Table 1.1 Unattended Communications Characteristics

MESSAGE-BASED	PUBLISHED-BASED
Customer Order Status*	
Customer (fax): What is the status of my order?	Customer (sign-in): Account balance, order status, tracking numbers, and other details display.
Service (email): I will check and get back to you.	Documentation and other supporting tools cross-reference what is important to this customer.
...Delay...	
Service (fax): It shipped.	
Customer (email): What is the tracking number?	
...Delay...	
Service (email): The tracking .... number is	

(continues)

Table 1.1 Unattended Communications Characteristics *(Continued)*

MESSAGE-BASED	PUBLISHED-BASED
Collecting Receivables	
Receivables (call): We are showing these invoices past due.	Receivables (call): We are showing these invoices past due.
Customer (call): I am missing the invoice.	Customer: I am missing the invoice.
Receivables (email): I will fax them.	Receivables: Sign-in at our site with this username and password. There you will see your open invoices.
Receivables (fax): Print and fax old invoices.	
Receivables (call): Did you receive the fax?	
Customer (call): OK	
Personal Contact	
Friend (call): Hi, how are you? Give me a call.	Friend (email): Hit your Web site last night. Great pictures of the soccer game. That video of saving the goal is awesome.
You (email): I am doing fine. Sorry I missed you. I am on the road.	• Having no email attachments preempts a major risk of virus attacks.
Friend (email): Could you email me the pictures of last week's soccer game?	• Known relationships receive known content.
You (email): Send pictures as email attachments.	
Friend (email): Opens attachments from email (allowing attachments is a virus risk).	
File Exchange	
Friend (call): I need this file.	Friend: Search your library.
You: Find the file in the recesses of your hard drive, reply to the message with attachments. Attachments might be duplicate, the wrong item, or infected with a virus.	If access is allowed, the file can download from your trusted site. In the near future is likely that no attachments will be accepted with email.

*Some 62% of customer service calls have to do with information about existing orders.

Serving answers saves your time and your customers' time and expands service to 24 hours a day, 7 days a week (24 x 7). Serving relationships from most desktops spreads the load and fine-tunes the response, changing the need for the buyer and seller to be mutually available (Figure 1.1) to information published 24x7 (Figure 1.2):

- A trading partner sees inventory levels, account balance(s), and order status.
- A vendor sees requests for quotes.
- Your child sees that you will make it to the game tonight.
- Your mom sees the latest digital movies of the grandchildren.

There is always an unlimited demand for better service and convenience for the customer and trading partner. Integrating communications into the physical operation of the business changes the entire flow of the sales process.

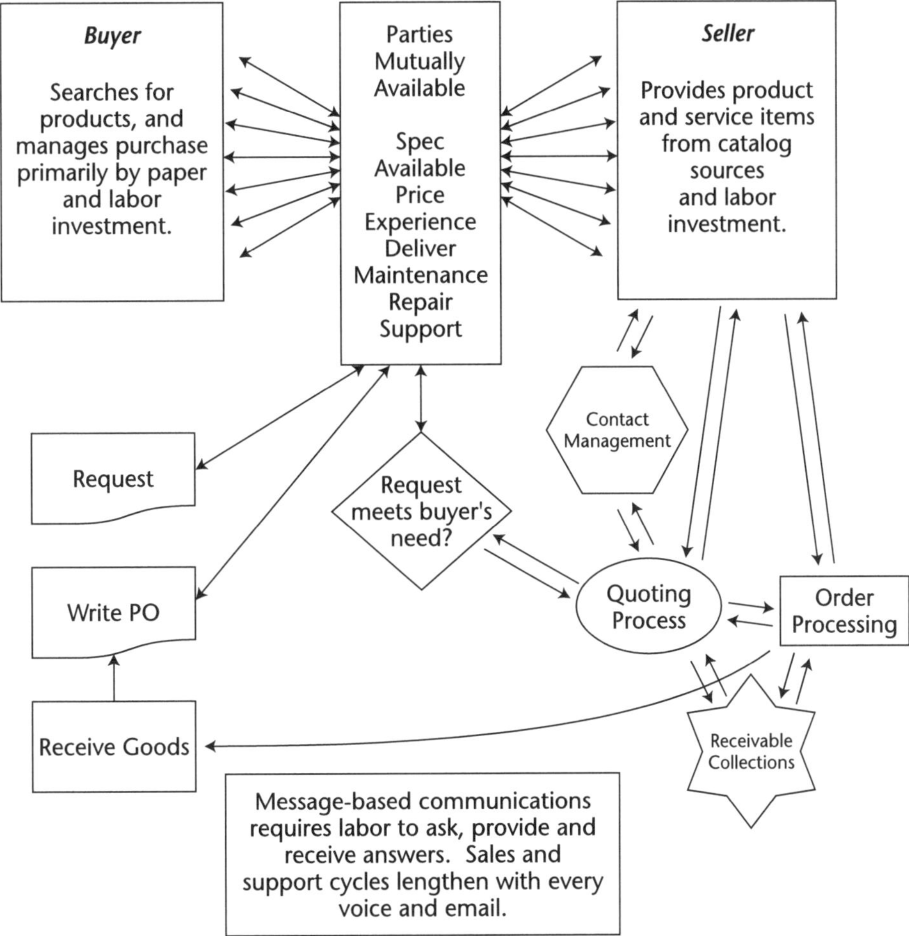

Figure 1.1 Message-based interactions between buyer and seller.

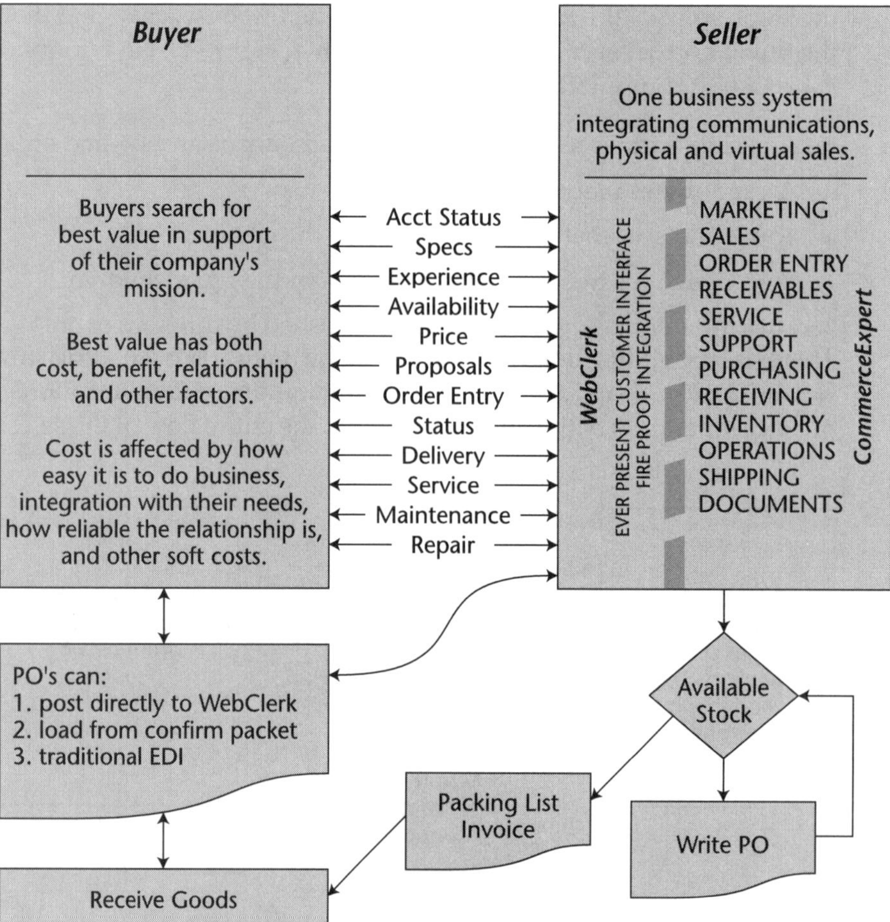

Figure 1.2 Publish-based interactions between buyer and seller.

For normal sales with established relationships, details are always available. Whenever buyers want to know details, they simply sign-in and their information is published to them. It is important to note that this is not a one-way street with only the buyer going to the seller's site. The seller may also go to the customer's site to see requests for quotes, project specifications, work order status, and project action reports. This interactive flow of communications mimics the way people relate. Historically, technology has limited our natural capability to multitask as we wait for replies to our messages. Published-based unattended communications eliminates this problem. A multiple exchange capability will also affect the way Web sites are designed. There is a tendency for companies to have a single Web site for managing Web communications, most likely due to inexperience and control issues. One Web site in a company is like having one telephone. You have a monolithic approach to the complex nature of communications. It is more competitive to have a Web interface supporting every relationship that profits from transacting with your company.

NOTE

By integrating servers into the structure of the physical business, Desktop Hosting expands the business logic that can be projected to your trading partners.

Because different tasks need to be accomplished by different people who have different capabilities, businesses put a phone on nearly every desk so the point of communication can be at the point of action. Centralizing the Web capability directly diminishes the expertise that is located at the point of action. By integrating servers into the structure of the physical business, Desktop Hosting expands the business logic that can be projected to your trading partners.

Nature of Networks

> *The compounded successes of Microsoft, FedEx, fax machines, and the Internet all hinge on the prime law of networks: Value explodes exponentially with membership, while this value explosion sucks in yet more members. The virtuous circle inflates until all potential members are joined. [emphasis added]*
>
> Kevin Kelly—"New Rules for the New Economy," *Wired* magazine, September 1997

It is not a profound observation to say that there has been dramatic progress in networking technology and that this progression will not stop. What can have profound business consequences is how you leverage this evolution to business advantage. The change from "Leave a message" to "Here's your answer" will build or destroy companies based on their ability to leverage this into a competitive advantage. Remember Wang, CDC, Cray, and others? Giants of the computer industry became irrelevant when their computing power did not adapt to the unattended intranet capabilities of providing "Here's your answer." The ants ate the elephants. Desktop Hosting is extending the power of "Here's your answer" to interacting with your trading partners, a network of networks.

Network Evolution

There has been a progression in microcomputer networks since the Macintosh was released in the mid 1980s. Mac users were rabid about their computers for two main reasons: the ability to create and the ability to effortlessly share that creativity across a local area network with everyone else in a workgroup. That instant-networking capability of the Mac went through a period of maturation until about 1990, when the price and reliability of 10BaseT EtherNet swept other microcomputer users into the network world. Figure 1.3 shows the progression of networks as they evolved over the past two decades.

Network Evolution

1990s IntraNets with SneakerNet to Extrnets

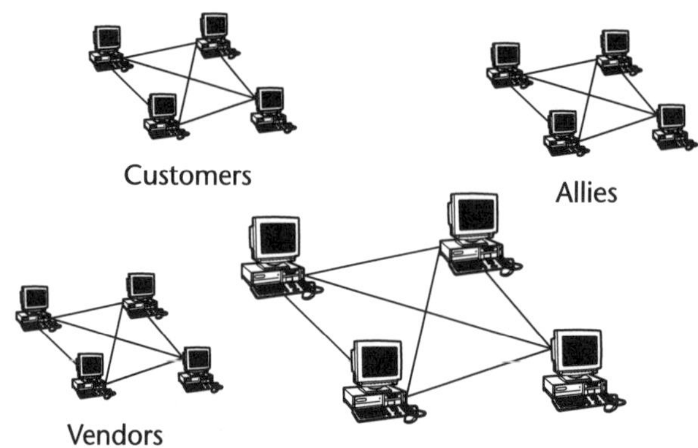

2000s Desktop Hosting Integrated Intra-Extra Nets

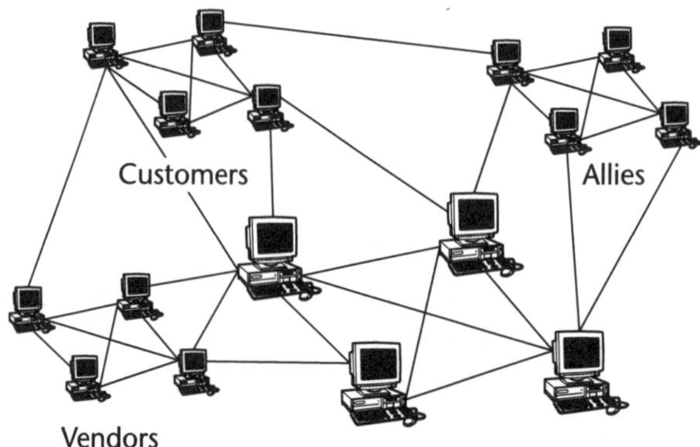

Figure 1.3 The evolution of network interactions.

With inexpensive network technology available, sneaker nets changed practically overnight into intranets. Computers changed from productivity tools to communications tools. Productivity toolmakers, like Wang, were swept from competitive existence when they could not adapt to the demand for communications capabilities. Microsoft's profits exploded as computers moved from a few desks to nearly everywhere in every company.

NOTE

Sneaker net is a manual data transport mechanism using people (sometimes wearing athletic shoes) carrying floppy disks from one computer to another.

The cycle is repeating. We have intranets in our companies. We have extranets with email and Web access. We have sneaker net between them. We physically copy messages between email applications and our customer service applications: manual transactions requiring multiple steps to accomplish a single task.

In 2001, Desktop Hosting completed its six-year gestation period. It has enough users to reach the tipping point, the point where the demand for integrated intranets and extranets operating from individual desktops will take on a life of its own. Over the next few years, business systems with these integrated communications, transaction processing, and customer service systems will flood into use. Remote, single-point e-commerce will fade as the relationships between salespeople and buyers, engineers and quality control, shipping and receiving, accounts payable and accounts receivable are managed from individual desktops. Relationship serving cannot be managed by remote control. A single remote site is usually better than nothing. But Desktop Hosting—data-driven, relationship-aware, dynamic, published-based, unattended communications—on everyone's desktop will sweep semiactive remote sites from competition.

Historical Examples

Centralizing technical resources is nothing new. At Honeywell in 1980, if you wanted to send a fax you had to prepare a paper document and take it to the hosting facility, thus paying someone to manage your unattended communications. In work areas Telex machines were used for most international communications. In 1985, fax machines were moved into work areas. The Telex stopped being used the next day, and every trading partner around the world bought a fax machine. There is great power in moving access to a communication device directly into the hands of the user.

Mainframe computing is another example. Until microcomputers swept the market, many companies leased mainframe computer time. Because of high capital costs and limited technical resources, mainframe hosting facilities evolved into an industry. When computing power moved to the desktop, these hosting facilities faded from their exclusive central status.

Remote hosting of Web sites will follow the demise of remote hosting for fax and computing power. When your company makes the change to extend your network to your trading partners may determine how competitive you are for the next decade.

Desktop Hosting: Catalyst for Networking Business Constituencies

The shift to Desktop Hosting will happen in the way that is traditional for networks: Over an extended gestation period early adopters refine the capabilities until a tipping point is reached. Past the tipping point, adoption cascades into an avalanche that destroys unsuspecting companies and propels those prepared into industry-leading status.

Hagel and Armstrong (1997) wrote an excellent book, *Net Gain—Expanding Markets Through Virtual Communities*, that outlines the history and speed with which networks expand. Figure 1.4 is a compilation of numbers from their findings; the curves are normalized to the y-axis so that all may be seen on the same vertical scale. In each of these cases, the networks grew slowly through a gestation periods and then exploded in membership when they reached their tipping points. If you act in advance of such a tipping point, your company can create a competitive advantage. I expect Desktop Hosting to be a catalyst for similar results among business constituencies that have a vested interest in networking. The individual curves in Figure 1.4 warrant specific discussion:

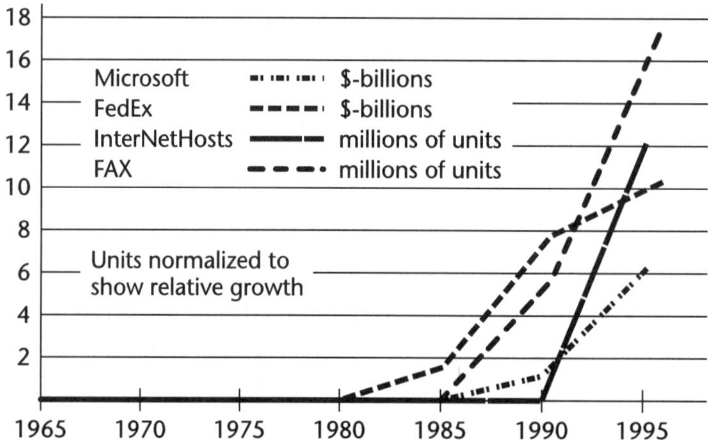

Figure 1.4 Networked entities have slow growth until the tipping point is reached. Thereafter, growth is explosive.

FedEx (light gray line) is a physical network. In about 1980, the concept of sending small packages with overnight delivery hit a tipping point and propelled FedEx into a brand that customers know and trust. The growth curve for FedEx is impressive. It would be even more so if FedEx's competitors had been more entrenched with other forms of shipment and had not jumped into the overnight delivery business.

Fax machines (dotted line) were commercially available in 1967. They suffered under a long gestation period, possibly due to the consumables and the centralized nature of companies, until widescale downsizing in the early 1980s. Out of sheer necessity, smaller companies acted to put the point of communication at the point of action by deploying fax machines into office areas. Fax use expanded.

Microsoft (dark gray line) and the InterNet Host (black line) both have the same tipping point in 1990. Microsoft did not cause this; it benefited from being in the right place at the right time.

In the late 1980s, computers were productivity tools. New purchases were justified based on the payback in labor savings for word processing and other tasks. During this period, other productivity tools such as Wang (word processing) or mainframe access (computing rental) were competitive. In the 1990s, networking technology came of age. Cheap, reliable, user-installable networking became universally available. Computers changed from being productivity tools to being communications devices. Wang failed. Control Data Corporation, Cray (super computers), and mainframe suppliers lost markets and faded from industry dominance to nonexistence. Microsoft became a giant as it was swept along.

The same pattern is about to happen in the world of Web hosting. It is approaching the tipping point that will annihilate centralized companies in favor of those that put the point of communications at the point of action. The tipping point seems to be triggered when a small percentage of potential users believe that the benefits of networking exceed the cost. This is an emotional or intellectual event that is accompanied by a drop in the cost of the communication tools. The cost of self-hosting is dropping radically, from approximately $1 million per site in 1998 to $849 in 2001 (and it is actually free on this book's accompanying CD-ROM).

Widescale use of the Web to network customers and vendors with a company's internal data is nearing the end of its gestation period. The cost of implementation has dropped dramatically. The floodgates of awareness are opening. How is your company going to compete when the tipping point is reached? How will you survive a radical change in customer expectations with current experience and capability?

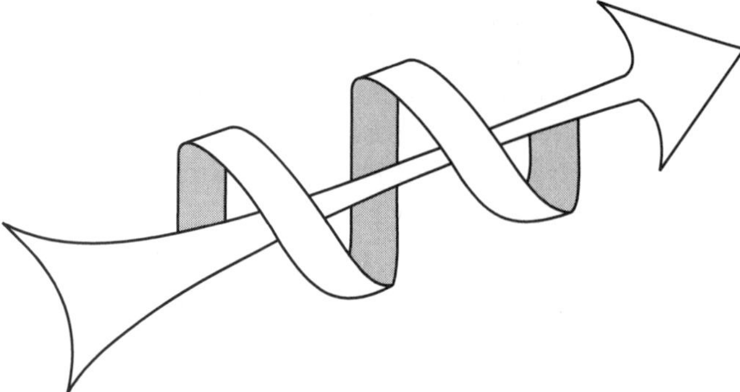

Figure 1.5 The Spiral of Excellence.

The Spiral of Excellence (Figure 1.5) is detailed in Chapter 2. Changing everything at once is not possible. Prepare for the tipping point by making iterative steps:

- Adhere to what you know.
- Test your assumptions.
- Technology is in flux. The primary task of a developer is to prepare for and adapt to this flux. Plan for change.
- Execute change. Implement cost-effective solutions before your competitors to provide an advantage.

CHAPTER 2

Principles of Desktop Hosting

This section outlines the basic assumptions on which this book is based. The assumptions are relatively simple:

- Buyers choose sellers.
- Competitive principles apply to business.
- Planning is required to achieve an objective.

Buyers Choose Sellers

People do business with their friends.

Mark H. McCormack—What They Don't Teach You at Harvard Business School (1984)

We act on emotion and justify with reason. We gather information to support a buying decision. We seek recommendations. But in the end, before we know a purchase is right for us, we have to commit. It is a pay-your-money, take-your-chances world.

In the buying decision, price is a factor, but only one factor. Look to your own buying habits. Do you buy regularly from the same source? Are you influenced by advertising and other brand-building activities? Have you bought milk or other items from a convenience store knowing it is 30 percent more expensive than a major grocery store? Price is a consideration, but we act on our judgment of what seems fair given the circumstances. Fair is a function of emotion.

I spent six years in a buying group for Honeywell's Defense Systems Division. The responsibilities of this group were to place contracts with outside manufacturers to support our production. We placed a wide array of subcontracts each year, some small and many for multiple millions of dollars. Vendor selection was always a primary concern because after we selected a vendor, we were committed and had little ability to meet schedules if failures occurred. Tooling had to be built, procedures implemented, and quality assured. We had to make buying decisions long before the impact of those decisions could be measured.

Under government contracts, accepting the low bidder was often required. Price was a hard-worked selection factor. Judgment was applied and vendors were qualified before price was considered. Risk could trump a great price even in the tightly regulated defense industry. I am now on the selling side of the buyer-seller relationship. It is even clearer that avoiding risks and unknowns drives buyers to select sellers in three circles (see Figure 2.1):

- Those they know and trust
- Those they know
- Others

From the buyer's perspective, known and trusted sellers are few, but they are close and fill most of the field of view.

Buyers often shop outside their trusted relationships, so it is incumbent on the seller to actively work to reassure the customers that value is being provided. If the price seems unfair, the quality poor, the service inadequate, or the value of the message poorly communicated, the value of the trusted relationship is discounted. If this discount is repeated, buyers change their habits and will establish a different trusted relationship. Desktop Hosting dramatically improves your ability to reassure your trusted relationships.

The dot.com companies were trustworthy and highly capitalized and had a lower operating cost than traditional retail companies. Logic indicates that by projecting this model in scale, they could capture entire markets. Technology allowed them to offer wider selections at lower prices. They could sell virtual inventory. But thus far, their business plans have failed more often than not. Their experience has two powerful lessons on opposite sides of the dot.com meltdown:

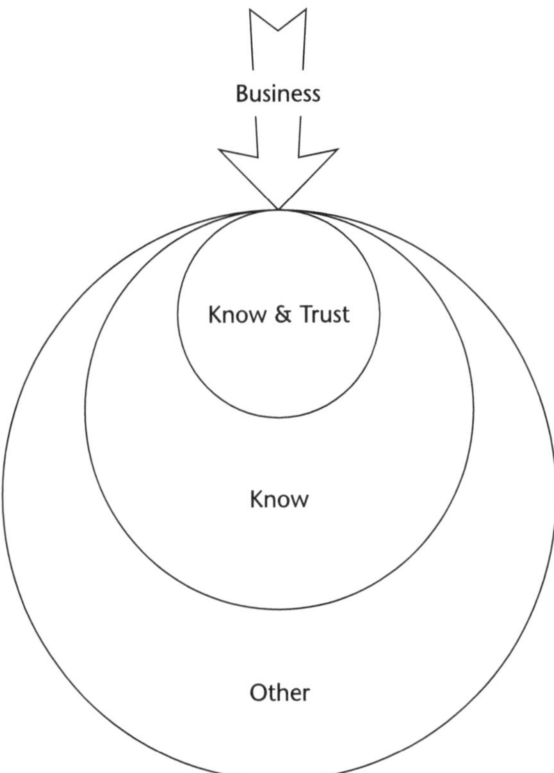

Figure 2.1 Circles of trust in business: Buyers choose sellers in three circles.

Failure side. Risks and unknown risks have nearly equal impact. Being trustworthy does not easily break existing trusted relationships. These companies did not establish enough sustained, trusted relationships before they burned through their capital.

Success side. Being better can dominate a market. The interactive customer service and virtual inventory offering of companies like Amazon.com are very powerful. They attract many shoppers. Amazon has had 29 million customers. Being available and interactive 24 hours a day, 7 days a week is beneficial to customers. Unanswered by traditional companies, this ability can secure market share and profitability.

Traditional companies providing Internet offerings and services can combine the best of both virtual and physical space. They can reinforce their existing trusted relationships with virtual inventory and interactive customer service. Part Two of this book walks you through improving unattended communications so you can publish order status, shipping information, product specifications, and service requests to existing customers. There are many factors involved in a sale. Price is almost always a factor. Convenience is a factor. But trusted relationships dominate.

Competitive Principles

The second major assumption of this book is that business is competitive. Winning in an uncertain competitive environment is aided by reviewing the military principles of war.[1] My belief in the usefulness of understanding these competitive principles is based on my experience in athletics, eight years as an infantry officer in the U.S. Army, and 20 years of building businesses. In many ways, business is ritualized combat where the winner is defined by survival and profitability. In these fast-changing times where demands on resources exceed availability, where decisions must be made before all the facts are known, understanding competitive principles of Objective, Simplicity, Economy of Force, and Mass aid in making adequate decisions with incomplete facts.

Objective

The objective of business is to increase profitable sales, where profit is the difference between the value paid by customers and the cost to compete.

Implementing concept: Be sales driven. Selling is the most critical process in any for-profit company. It triggers customer understanding of the value provided, and triggers commitment to buy and satisfaction with paying for the value your company delivers. Align technology policy to support increasing profitable sales and communication tools reinforcing the selling process

The selling process extends from a company's marketing effort to the customer's check clearing at the bank. It involves everyone in your company whose activities add to the customer's understanding of value that should be paid for or affects costs. In other words, it includes vendors, employees, and even shareholders. Uniting the diverse interests of these groups and the individuals within them requires clearly stated objectives of who does what, why, when, and where.

Simplicity

Simplicity is attainable. Drive out sources of variation and multiple systems that must be both managed and coordinated.

[1] For more on the principles of war, I recommend the book *War, Power and Politics* - selections from *On war* and *I believe and profess* by Karl von Clausewitz (1780-1831). Selections were translated to English and published by Chicago, Regnery [1962].

Implementing concept: Integrate your intranet and extranet systems into a single business system. In many companies today the Web site is not integrated into the company's internal selling process. Creating two separate business systems, one physical and one e-commerce, significantly increases the complexity of keeping the systems aligned. Desktop Hosting changes this so the physical and virtual business systems are aspects of each other.

Economy of Force

Tailor effort to need.

Implementing concept: Drive the cost of transactions toward zero by making communications an integral part, not separate from the selling process. Implement solutions that are affordable to implement and affordable to maintain. Subordinate technology and other processes to the needs of the selling process.

Mass

There is power in empowering everyone.

Implementing concept: Many hands make light work. Network everyone into your business process. Think commerce, not e-commerce. Your company does not have just one telephone; you put a phone on every desk so your employees can conveniently communicate with your trading partners. Desktop Hosting extends your current attended efforts to put the point-of-communication at the point-of-action to unattended communications.

Approach to Using These Principles

Power and Excellence provide an approach to implementing competitive principles. At my company we use the graphic in Figure 2.2 to put this approach into action.

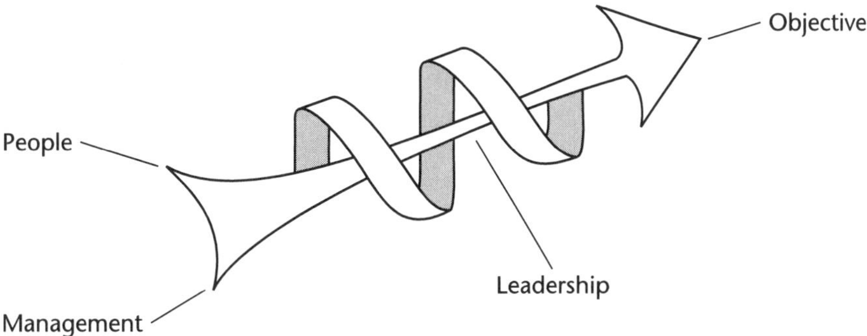

Figure 2.2 The Spiral of Excellence demonstrates power and excellence.

Power

Power is the will and ability to win applied to achieving an objective.
Karl von Clausewitz[2]

- One fork of the tail is the will to win. This is your people: their creativity, intelligence, labor, time, and effort.
- The other fork of the tail is management, the allocation of resources and training.
- Leadership is the shaft. Leadership is what gives these diffused, self-interested components a unifying and clearly defined objective. Communications is the aspect of leadership that clarifies an understanding of the objective and each individual's responsibility to achievement of the objective.
- The objective—the arrow head—is who does what, why, when, and where. Measurable steps toward company goals.

Excellence

Excellence is the process of relentlessly improving.

The spiral represents Excellence:

Begin by adhering to what you know (the first point on the spiral). Consistency provides a base from which to evaluate current efforts and the effects of change. Recognize that consistency in itself is not power or excellence. By its very nature, excellence is a failure to comply with standards. The drive for standards is often equated to the drive for uniformity—stifling efforts and people that do not conform, even if that nonconformity is a more viable path to excellence.

Test your assumptions (90 degree rotation). Examine what is good and bad about what you do. Look at basic assumptions, not just ongoing activities.

Plan to change your organization (90 degree rotation). Recognize that any time you change an organization, you will precipitate a crisis.

Pull the trigger (90 degree rotation). Execute the plans and implement the crisis.

[2] Karl von Clausewitz (1780-1831) was a Prussian Field Marshall at the time of Napoleon. Read War, Power and Politics to understand much of the reasoning behind this definition of power.

Repeat the cycle, refining your experience, and reinforcing an understanding of your objectives and goals. Home in on what is really important. Approaching excellence as a process encourages you to begin, to iterate, to refine, and to adapt.

Get Started

The hardest part about beginning is getting started.

In a new arena, how do you begin without a perfected vision of where you want to end up? Without experience in an area, how do you correctly define what you want to achieve? Our answer is to take your best guess, write a clear statement of the objective as you know it, then jump in with affordable resources. Gain experience. Use that experience to adjust to where you want to end.

In marksmanship training, the first step is to start shooting. The second step is to consistently hit the same part of the target by aiming at the bull's eye. The third step is to adjust the sights of the weapon so the bullets hit the bull's eye. The same approach applies to business.

Start by beginning. State the objective and start shooting.

Adjust to Target

The target changes with market conditions and competitive actions. Waiting for a clear picture of the future sacrifices the experience that could have been gained by acting today.

Implement leadership techniques that encourage your employees to continually reevaluate your assumptions, to be involved in adjusting the many aspects of adding value that makes a company competitive. The objective defines the "bull's eye," adjusting the tasks of each person has to be distributed to the point-of-action, the person that has to get each job done.

Planning to Win

To be powerful in your markets, every component—people, resources, leadership, and communications—needs to be an integral part of every aspect and change in your business. The importance of integrated communications cannot be understated. The current selling of e-solutions separate from a company's primary business is generally a disservice.

Plan for This Book

The following outlines the plan for this book using the preceding format:

Objective. The objective of this handbook is defined by:

- Who: Bill James and John Wiley & Sons.
- What: Publish the defining concept that makes the Web a profitable business tool for the average business.
- Where: In Wiley's existing markets.
- When: By mid-2002.
- Why: To create the Desktop Hosting market, increasing Wiley's sale of the book, JITCorp's sales of software, and readers' profitable sales from using the book and software.

The intent of this book is to provide clarity, concepts, and then implementation for unattended communications. Plans are based on the following format (those from the military may recognize this as the format for the five-paragraph field order):

Objective. Who, What, Why, When, Where?

Background. What helps? Hinders? What are the general conditions?

Execution. How the objective is to be achieved?

Logistics and Finance. Resources required to achieve the objective.

Communications. Coordinating activities.

Integrated communications is a key aspect of the leadership required to bring an organization through times of competitive challenges. I will use this format throughout the book to help communicate with you. I recommend that you use the same format to communicate within your organization.

Background

Customer Focus. Profit comes from trading with someone who is willing to buy from you at a price greater than your cost to compete. Communications develops the customer's appreciation of the value they should pay for.

Better Service. Being "known and trusted" has great competitive advantages. In all businesses, not everything is perfect. Desktop Hosting provides a means of publishing to customers the current status at the customer's convenience. Integrating your customer into your selling process strengthens your competitive position as "known and trusted." Instead of "Leave a message" you provide "Here's your answer."

Profit versus Technology. Successful business is about being profitable, not about technology. Empowering your customers, vendors, and employees to buy, sell, and service via the Web expands the "known and trusted" relationship. Putting the point-of-communications at the point-of-action assures everyone that the right answer will be available on demand any time of day or night. Information Services can drive technology to support their company's selling process.

Message-Based Communications. Unattended communication is traditionally message-based. Each customer request requires them to invest labor. The message often goes to someone who must invest labor to research the correct answer and invest labor to respond. Each labor-based transaction adds costs, increases probabilities of failure to respond, and decreases value. In the selling process each message delay lengthens the sales cycle and diminishes the "trusted" relationship.

Published-Based Communications. Database-driven business systems manage data so that as people do their jobs, the data changes. When the shipping person sends a package, an invoice is created, the order decrements, shipping charges are calculated, the label is printed, and inventory adjusts. In doing their jobs, the data changes. Integrating this data with Desktop Hosting makes the customer an integral part of your support system. Important details are published. No labor is invested in reporting.

Desktop Hosting. Put the point-of-communication at the point-of-action. It integrates unattended communications into your physical business operations and your relationship with your customers, employees, and vendors.

Execution

Change the standard for unattended communication from message- to publish-based. The following list outlines specific actions to attain publish-based interactions:

- Read book
- Install WebClerk
- Take orders, service, and purchase on the Web
- Build experience
- Modify sites to meet needs
- Build experience
- Open transactions to trading partners

Logistics and Finance. Drive the cost of achieving the objective toward zero by providing a free, full version of our Desktop Hosting software program with the book.

Communications. Communications is provided by four sources:

- Written instructions contained in the book and in the interactive documentation provided with the WebClerk application on the accompanying CD.
- Movies provided with the training CD. These are also provided free with this book.
- Interactive forums at www.webclerk.com and www.desktophosting.com for our programs and for the Desktop Hosting industry in general.
- Purchasable support from our tech support group, available at www.webclerk.com.

CHAPTER 3

Planning to Win

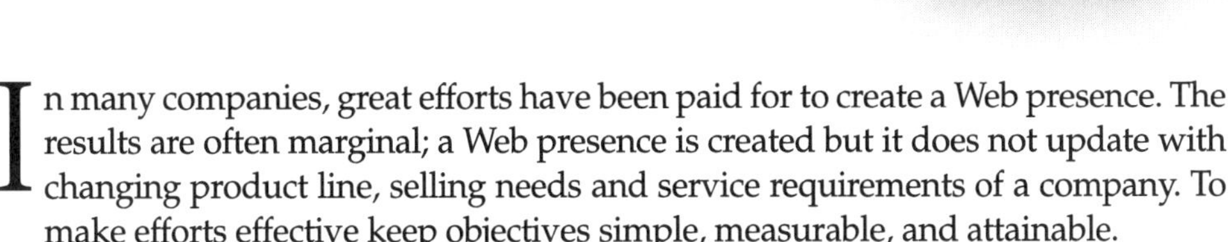

In many companies, great efforts have been paid for to create a Web presence. The results are often marginal; a Web presence is created but it does not update with changing product line, selling needs and service requirements of a company. To make efforts effective keep objectives simple, measurable, and attainable.

As an example of an attainable objective, let's walk through an example of planning and implementing the technology to take Web-based orders.

The Exercise

The following exercise inducts you into the world of Desktop Hosting.

Objective

The objective is to take a sales order via the Web, from your computer, using demo data provided so that you build experience necessary to stay competitive on the Web. This will take about 10 minutes.

Who: You

What: Take a sales order via the Web

Where: On your computer using demo data provided

When In the next 10 minutes

Why: To build experience necessary to stay competitive on the Web

Background

A full, single-user version of WebClerk is on the enclosed CD. This software is a comprehensive sales and operations software program with built-in Web serving abilities. Installing this program also installs the prefabricated Web site and a demo data set that is properly set up. It is a good idea to use this demo data set when learning the program.

Execution

Use the WebClerk application on the CD that accompanies this book to place an order via the Web to your computer. Specific steps are listed here.

1. Install the WebClerk application.
2. Make sure you have no other Web server running on the local machine.
3. There are several ways for browsers to behave based on how they are configured. Typically you do not have to worry about how your machine is configured if your access to the Internet is via a router. If you have a dial-up modem, when you launch the WebClerk you may have some interactions with your modem to connect to the outside Web.
4. Launch the WebClerk application. At the password window, click on the second choice and then click on the OK button. The program will open to the WebClerk Flow window.
5. Click on the Launch WebClerk button on the center left. This will launch the WebClerk Web server.
6. Launch your browser application.
7. In your browser, enter the address http://localhost or http://127.0.0.1. These addresses are the defaults for your local machine (unless there is a proxy server which controls this address). If your browser does not display the demo Web site, specify the IP address for your machine. Read the TechNote Browser Options and/or watch the movie on the CD BrowerOption.mov.
8. Click on the Catalog URL on the left-side navigation frame. The Web page for the catalog will display.

9. Click on the Kayak URL. A list of kayaks will display.
10. Enter a quantity in a few of the fields.
11. Click on the Submit button. The items will be added to your shopping cart.
12. Click on Sign-in URL on the left-side navigation frame. A default username and password are provided.
13. Click on Submit button. You will be signed in as Terra with James Integrated Technologies. The screen will show your open account balance for all unpaid invoices and unapplied payments.
14. Click on the CheckOut URL. A page for confirming your order will display.
15. Click on the Submit button without modifying any of the fields. In future exercises, I will walk you through changing zip codes, carriers, tax jurisdictions, and other options.
16. Your completed order will display in your browser. Note the order number.
17. Bring WebClerk application to the front. Go to the Review Menu and select CommerceExpert Flow. A window shows the features of the integrated sales and operations software.
18. Click on the WorkFlow button in the lower center of the Production window. A list of open orders will display. Find your order number in the third column. Click on the line, and the order lines will display. Double-click on the line to display the full order. From here you can process the order, change status, assign work orders, issue purchase orders, and accomplish many other tasks required to complete the transaction. There are exercises for managing orders on the CD.

Hardware

No special equipment is required. Computer requirements are a current Macintosh or Windows operating system running on a computer with at least 128 megabytes of RAM and at least 100 megabytes of available hard drive space.

Communications

Descriptions of ways to link your company to the Internet are beyond the scope of this book—and they change constantly. Descriptive instructions about communications options are available in WebClerk's TechNotes. These may be accessed in a number of ways:

- Look under the Review menu >> TechNote References. Enter First Web Order in the Name field and hit the Tab key to display the detailed instructions. There are additional Learning Exercises in the TechNotes.
- In the subject field of the TechNote Reference window, list the TechNotes by typing "Learning Exercises" and then hitting the Tab key.

Summary

As you gain experience, your objectives may be expanded to incorporate customer service, work orders to coordinate activities, shipment tracking, order status, business-to-business (B2B) conduits, proposals, inventory levels, virtual inventory, and many other tasks for which there are specific training lessons in this book and on the accompanying CD. Chapter 7, "Case Studies," has additional exercises within the case studies.

Background

If you have completed the preceding exercise, you have booked a sales order using your computer as your interactive server. Welcome to Desktop Hosting. Before we go into more exercises, we will look at additional background information so that you can better plan how to deploy your resources. There is power in using the Web well, and there may be failure in applying it incorrectly.

General Situation

The Web is a powerful tool for providing customer service and an easier buying experience for your customers. Amazon.com embraces the concepts of interacting with customers, providing them what they want at a time they want it, with interactive support during the process. Amazon.com has been rewarded with incredible customer service approval ratings. Figure 3.1 shows that its customer satisfaction is consistently high. Amazon.com has also spent $2 billion to build its base. Wine.com burned through $600 million and was recently liquidated in bankruptcy. WebVan.com and many others have also failed.

So how does your company embrace a radical change in communications without billions of spare dollars in the midst of commercial failure by companies with seemingly unlimited capital? How do you design an approach that affordably integrates the power of the Web into your sales, service, and operations?

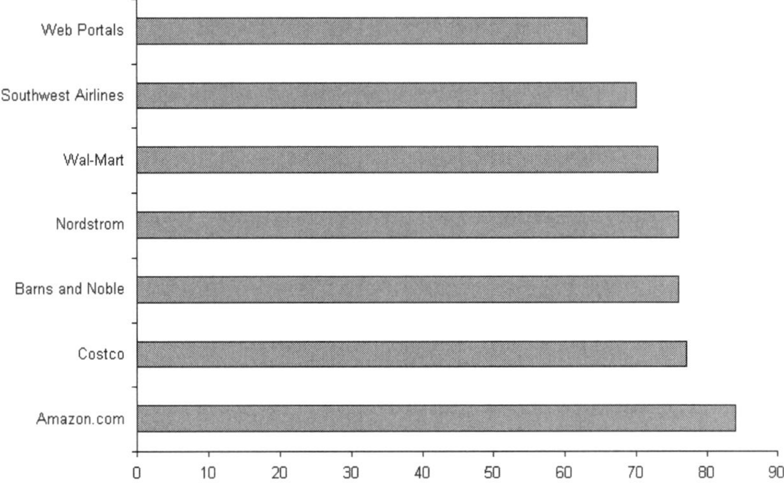

Figure 3.1 Amazon's customer satisfaction index.

Start with What You Know

Design for simplicity. What is simple can be achieved with two steps:

- Start with what you know. Build from and for your existing customer base.
- Make communications an integral part of your operations.

The intent of Desktop Hosting is to publish the correct information to the correct person at the time of the request. No longer should a request wait for an answer; an answer is supplied at the time of asking. A user should be able to sign in and receive status on the account balance, open orders, recent shipments, current pricing, user instructions, and so on. The trend toward making such information available via the Web is growing, but most current Web sites are only marketing sites, not sales and service access points. They provide standard answers but nothing about the details that keep relationships together among trading partners.

Your existing customers are the ones who will most appreciate it if you improve their ability to transact with you. Direct your first efforts at them.

Simplicity and Mass

Because of the number of transactions made every hour of every day by every employee, customer, and vendor, designing a system to manage every task is like eating an elephant—it is an overwhelming endeavor. There are two strategies for tackling this:

Create an elephant-eating monster. Build a system that is so large that the mass of an elephant seems like lunch. This was the approach taken by many members of the dot.com meltdown. Elephant-eating monsters are hard to build, hard to handle, and not very adaptable.

Small bites, lots of friends. Excite the self-interest of everyone involved. Spread the advantages and the work across all those who can benefit from having their transactions communicated among their trading partners. This is the approach taken by this book, and it can be repeated within a company and applied to the supply chain of entire industries.

It is simple. Simplicity is achievable. It is massive. Within your company, when you spread an effort across all your people, it becomes more achievable. The old adage that "many hands make light work" is applicable.

External to your company, the same principle applies. Your trading partners and competitors share similar problems. Designing your network to interact with your trading partners and customers expands your ability to compete. When every bookseller can use Amazon.com to sell virtual inventory; to provide customer service 24 hours a day, seven days a week; and to notify customers of other products of interest to him or her, Amazon will be less of a juggernaut. This same concept is applicable to nearly every business. Amazon takes excellent care of its customers around the clock. If you do not, or you cannot, and some competitor in your market space can, you will be faced with hard choices.

Implementing Transaction Technology

Companies like Amazon and FedEx spend million of dollars to put rich data and transaction capabilities into their sites and to keep it current. In their respective 2000 annual reports, Amazon.com says it spent $269 million on technology and content expenses alone, and FedEx (a capital-intensive operation) spent $378 million on information and technology equipment.

Table 3.1 lists typical problems that occur when implementing transaction technology and describes solutions to the problems in generic terms.

Table 3.1 The Big Six Problems with Implementing Transaction Technology

PROBLEM	SOLUTIONS
Obtaining stable, understandable technology.	Wide-market software programs are coming of age, replacing internal development as the primary source for these applications. Many of these standardized programs have survived their Version 1.0 blues and are viable in the industries applying them.
Getting—and keeping—your data in the application so it may be used.	Small companies prosper in the same way ants eat elephants; small bites, lots of friends.
Data conversion continues to be a major obstacle. Managing it is still an art form.	Many businesses share the same data and technology problems as their allies and competitors. A common-solution, common-tools, common-data, common-language solution networks weak single companies into a Fortune One entity. Sabre provides such a common-language for travel agents to sell airplane seats. FTD has done something similar for florists. This commercial library of products we have named "common-language." It is explained more fully at the end of this chapter. Extend your network so that the very transactions that currently support your business become interactive content tailored to the needs of your customers and provide opportunities to your vendors. Change from message-based unattended communications to publish-based ones. Desktop Hosting expands your network so that transactional data is shared with and services your trading partners.
Keeping your data current once it is loaded.	Library services will develop, such as provided by Sabre for airplane seats.
Pricing, tax jurisdictions, shipping costs, and much other data decay quickly. It is generally too expensive for individual companies to keep all this up-to-date.	Subscribing to such a data set spreads the cost of maintaining data across many companies.
Training your people to use the technology with your data.	Web-based training, multimedia, and other tools are available online to assist with training. Specific Tools we use are listed in Chapter 7.

(continues)

Table 3.1 The Big Six Problems with Implementing Transaction Technology *(Continued)*

PROBLEM	SOLUTIONS
Making the technology work with your trading partners.	EDI, XML, and other translation technologies are in place. They translate data in one company's business program to a format usable by another. XML is much more fluid than EDI. These are usable but complex tools. I believe the common-language concept will be far more viable as Desktop Hosting develops in the market.
Keeping the technology working with your trading partners.	EDI has momentum and is still being forced on vendors by major buyers. It remains expensive and unstable (definition: changing faster than is easily maintained). XML is a much better translation technology. Again, the common-language approach exemplified by Sabre is less expensive and a more dynamic means of adjusting to the constantly changing common data.

Design for Your Type of Business

The Web makes it possible to drive the cost of transactions toward zero. Those cost savings provide a competitive advantage to the companies that implement Web hosting first, implement it profitably, and gain the most market share in this new economy. This was the premise of the dot.com companies, but they failed in large numbers despite having so much capital at their command because there were fundamental design flaws in their concepts.

Why Pigs Don't Fly

There are more design parameters for success than to lower the cost of operation. Like companies, pigs don't fly because the pressures of competition and the requirements for them to excel in their particular niches have tailored their current structures. Reality terminates those that spend effort on nonprimary tasks. When resources are limited, survival depends on focusing resources on primary capabilities required to win in your niche. The same is true of business structures. Different business structures develop by amplifying successful characteristics. They evolve by filling competitive niches. They must be very good at their primary task; spending effort on secondary tasks can cost their survival.

> *Bishop's Rule: Assumption is the mother of all screw-ups.*
>
> Lt. Dan Bishop*
>
> *Dan was one of my platoon leaders when I was an Infantry company commander in Alaska (his phrasing was actually a little more colorful!)

Like a gold rush, the Web was so exciting that people from every walk of life swept in to stake a claim on it. As is typical, many applied their experience and judgment; this is good. They sometimes did it without examining the assumptions upon which their experience and judgement were based; this is dangerous. The results of accepting unmodified assumptions as true in a different environment lead to observations such as Bishop's Rule.

Assumptions that work well in one business structure are detriments to the ability to survive in other niches. In the rush to the Web, it was assumed that if enough money was invested, capital business structures could be applied to supply chains, disenfranchising the current structure of business, creating unbelievable returns to those who destroyed the old. Pigs do not fly because it was not essential to the evolution of their structure. Capital structures cannot replace supply chains because of the fundamental natures that have evolved over time and in response to competitive pressures.

Supply Chain Structures

Supply chain structures are the network of companies that survive based on getting value to customers with the least consumption or lowest cost of raw materials. Table 3.2 describes their typical composition.

Table 3.2 Characteristics of Supply Chain Business Structures

SUPPLY CHAIN STRUCTURE	EXAMPLES	EXPERTISE REQUIRED	SOURCE OF REVENUE/ SURVIVABILITY
Producers	Manufacturers, miners, farmers	Companies that add value to raw materials. They compete by adding more value to the raw materials relative to the cost or amount of raw materials consumed.	Add the most value while consuming the least value raw materials.
Transporters	Distributors, wholesalers, sales reps	Companies that add value to raw materials. They compete by adding more value to the raw materials relative to the cost or amount of raw materials consumed.	Sell items with the best margin relative to the cost of selling, delivering, and supporting.
Supporters	Retail	Relationships with, knowledge about, and support of end users.	Proximity, known and trusted.

Capital Structures

Capital structures are composed of companies that moderate the cyclical swings experienced by supply chain companies. An example is the farmer, who must have land, buy seed, plant that seed, and harvest, process, and sell the crop before collecting for the effort. Sometimes storms wipe out an entire crop and the cycle extends. To avoid this, supply chain companies pay capital companies to fund efforts or to hedge against uncertainty; the capital companies risk their money for a portion of the value that is added by supply chain companies.

To moderate these great swings, capital structures evolved. Money is invested, and the expectation is that it will be consumed. At some later date, the investment is expected to pay back at a rate relative to the risk (number of failures) of that type of investment. Table 3.3 describes the typical composition of capital structures.

In summary, if you want your company to win, focus on your core competitive requirements. Know yourself and the parameters of your competitive environment. Rules that apply well in one set of circumstances may fail in yours. If flying is your niche, strive to be extraordinary. If you root for nuts and berries, do not waste valuable resources trying to grow wings. Prefixing an e does not change the nature of an industry or the companies that have evolved to fill the niche.

Table 3.3 Characteristics of Capital Business Structures

CAPITAL STRUCTURE	EXAMPLES	EXPERTISE REQUIRED	SOURCE OF REVENUE/ SURVIVABILITY
Venture	Hobby, family, angles, venture funds	Personal relationship between the high-risk/ highly creative source and established successful companies/markets that might benefit from the source being successful	Funds and expertise applied to incubate ideas and people into companies that produce capital gains
Banks and equity-based lenders	Banks and equity-based lenders	Ability to minimize risk to themselves and skill in penalizing their customers who do not perform as expected	Small percentage gain applied over time
Exchanges (equity and futures)	Stock markets, boards of trade	Ability to manage a massive number of transactions such that those they manage the transactions for are pleased that a general public awareness is created	Very small fee per transaction, multiplied by very many individual transactions

Know Survival Characteristics

By some estimates, more than 1,000 such e-marketplaces—for products that ranged from commodities such as lumber to specialized components such as airplane parts—managed to receive funding. Unfortunately, most of these companies failed to realize that the lifeblood of a marketplace is liquidity, and that, in B2B, a few large enterprises can generate most of the transaction volume so critical for that purpose.

*These behemoths typically don't need the help of an independent marketplace, however, and they can bargain fiercely with anyone who hopes to trade with them. Independent, fee-based marketplaces have therefore mostly languished in the absence of a business model that could vindicate their early optimism.**

*From the McKinsey Quarterly, March 26, 2001, 4:00 a.m. PT
http://news.cnet.com/news/0-1007-201-5223390-0.html

The dot.com failures have little to do with the Web being a spectacular tool and a lot to do with trying to make pigs fly. People from the venture capital and traditional capital business world applied assumptions that work for capital companies to supply chain companies. The thought was that online exchanges were going to sweep aside distributors and retailers. Massive capital was dumped in, but customers did not leave their known and trusted suppliers to comply with the new model.

Buyers have near zero tolerance for failure. Price is not as important as the total costs to buy and use a product and to manage the risk of buying. Exchanges can manage trades on known commodities but not the nuances that make or break a buy. As an example, as a buyer for Honeywell, I once needed 7 million pounds of 6061 aluminum alloy of a specific size and quality to build cartridge cases for the A10 aircraft under a three-year, fixed-price contract with the U.S. government. To protect against price changes, we bought a futures contract at an exchange for aluminum.

Aluminum futures are a capital structure trade. I bought the right to buy 7 million pounds of aluminum at some future date at a specific price. What type of aluminum was not specified. As we needed the actual aluminum, we sold this right to buy aluminum at the fixed price at a gain or loss depending on the price change in aluminum. This gain or loss approximately offset our true loss or gain in buying the actual aluminum that met all our specifications from our trusted trading partner, Kaiser.

The financial transaction at the exchange was used to abate a price risk in the actual purchase of the real aluminum. We would never have purchased unspecified aluminum from an unspecified source for the actual build. The supply chain transaction assured use of excellent material that met our specific needs and manageable risk. The rules for the capital and supply chain transactions were radically different.

Creating an exchange that can vertically integrate a supply chain is at least unlikely. There are too many specifics. There is too much fear and risk of failure to let specifics go undefined. This handbook will help you to put these specifics in your unattended communications. It will give you experience in knitting your trading partners into a network that exchanges these details without the repetitive labor and delays of sending messages and waiting for them to be received, interpreted, and replied to.

Tailor your capabilities to fill the needs of your type of business. To obtain the competitive advantages offered by the Web, extend these capabilities to those that know and trust you; design your communications to match the needs of your trading partners. Ways to tailor unattended communications within your business are defined in Chapter 5, "Getting a Project Funded, Keeping It Funded." In that chapter, the benefits of it to various functions in your company are highlighted. The idea is that by directly aligning technology efforts with improved sales, you can get projects off the ground and keep them running.

Find Allies

Integrating an entire industry in a capital structure did not work. Making exchanges to handle the data translations did not work. What has worked is to "intellectually" integrate the many companies in a supply chain with a common-language. Sabre has done this for the travel industry. They created a data library that many companies can use to trade constantly changing inventories.

Most companies in most industries share a common problem. Data decays faster that it can be affordably maintained. Sources, availability, pricing, lead times and many other key data points in selling are constantly in flux. As Desktop Hosting expands, this common problem of data decay will be met by a common-solution of Virtual-Inventory, Common-Language, Common-Tools, and Common-Data. A library of data can be created and maintained that meets the needs of most like businesses. Filters can be applied to fine-tune this data to special needs. Updating the data via the Web permits every business to use the data locally for managing transactions.

The library has authorized access to common elements of a subscriber's data set that permits it to gather and publish specific data. Details such as item number, price, and availability are gathered and distributed to existing and potential trading partners in conjunction with the rule sets defined by both the publisher and the subscriber, such as:

General filters. Some of these filters are based on known industry factors such as climate, geography, population, niche markets, and so on. These filters can be applied by central librarians.

Relationship filters. These filters are applied between trading partners to modify the common data to their specific relationship. Published catalogs, terms, and policies are tailored to relationships.

Opt-in filters. These give notifications of changes in data.

A key design parameter for our Common-Language efforts is that the cost of the data and systems to use it must be less than the cost savings provided by the effort. Figure 3.2 illustrates the library functions of Common-Language where input comes from many points and is distributed for local use based on the profiles defined by the users. Information flows in both directions. Unlike an exchange, all transactions are independently communicated between the specific trading partners. The SKUs, cross references to suppliers, and product details are posted into each trading partner's databases, keeping current the language in which they transact.

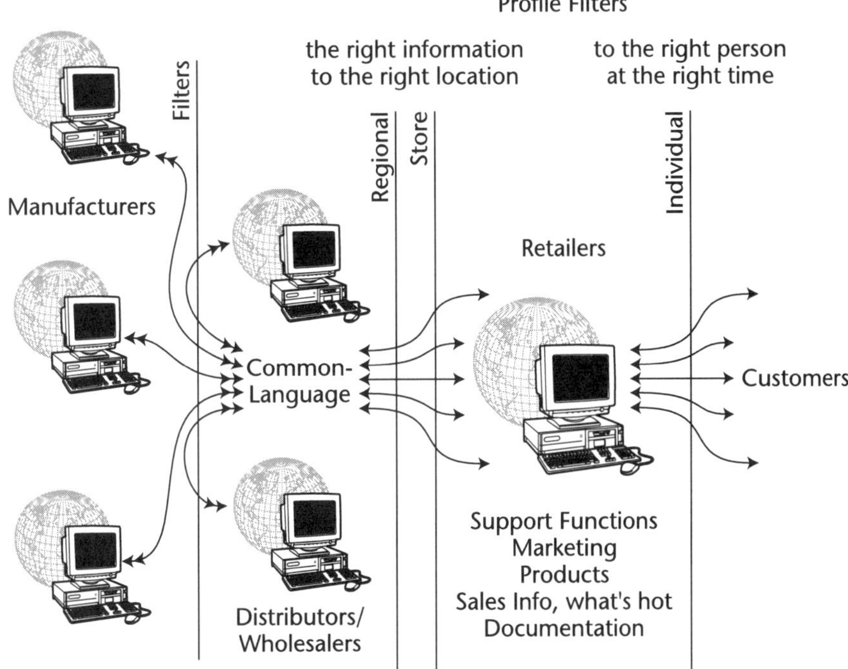

Figure 3.2 Library functions of the Common-Language.

Design Considerations for the Common-Language Approach

The Common-Language approach to industries basically applies Deming principles and statistical process control (SPC) techniques to the selling process. To make the communication process more repeatable, drive out sources of variation. Trading partners typically have business systems that do not treat data the same way. Even the same products can have different part numbers, descriptions, and other variations between partners. EDI and XML are translation technologies that have been developed to help translate between companies who must trade but speak different "languages." Figure 3.3 shows how complex it is for trading partners to translate data between their islands of technology and data. Difficulties are multiplied as the number of trading partners increase.

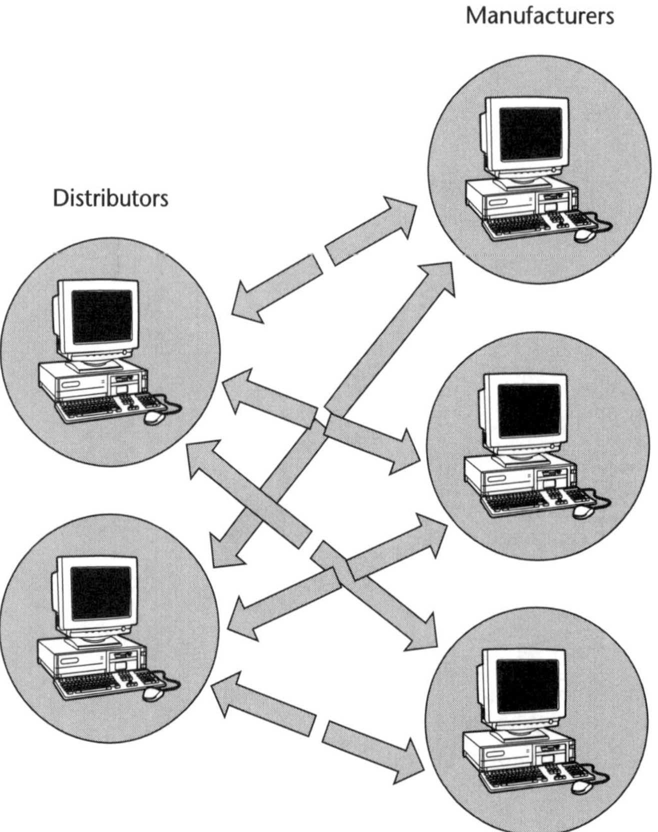

Figure 3.3 Manufacturers and distributors.

This difference between these languages is compounded because data decays faster than most companies maintain it. In many companies, key data perishes and has to be rebuilt every time it is used. Even when up to date, data provided by a trading partner is often in a format that is different from what can be directly used

This constant decay of data is a common problem. It has a common solution.

Common Data

Data is changing all the time for business details such as pricing, availability, engineering changes, marketing materials, and so on. Many trading partners that receive this data lack the resources to assimilate it into the way that they communicate with their customers and even internal staffs. I have talked with small engine manufacturers. They have worked hard to provide their data to their supply chain partners on CDs. The result: The mechanic in the field has 30 CDs that he does not have time to load because he has to fix engines.

Data can be better managed across an industry if it is viewed by its nature. In Figure 3.4 I have divided data into three, possibly oversimplified, classes:

Proprietary data. This is the core of your business and contains details regarding with whom and how you do business. This data should be highly protected.

Transactional data. This details transactions with trading partners. It only exists when shared with a partner. Unless you treat every trading partner exactly the same, it needs to be protected from public knowledge.

Common data. This is the data you must publish to your general marketplace in order to compete. This is typically a catalog of products and services, general terms and conditions, and other trade policies and procedures.

Each of these major data types has variations. For instance, you want your catalog of products to be available to those with whom you trade. However, you may wish to have different prices, terms, and conditions for wholesale trade than those for retail. You may limit the geography in which you trade. Or sales and accounting departments may have different transactional data for the same customer.

Unattended communications systems can adequately publish your common data within the rules required. It must also protect the transactional and proprietary data at the appropriate security level. Table 3.4 outlines the nature and protection required for general data types. As you look at it, note that data can change categories: A secret alliance or deal may shift from proprietary to common. One day it is a closely guarded secret. The next day it is the center of a massive public relations effort.

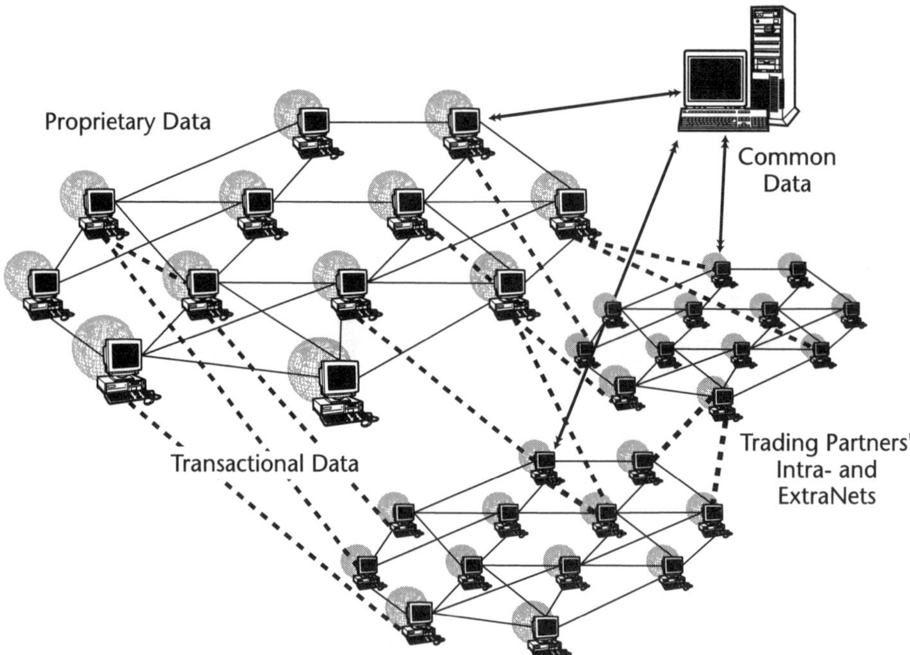

Figure 3.4 Types of data dynamically networked.

Design criteria should account for how data should be used. Sometimes vital proprietary data is left completely open, or technocrats lock useful data with unnecessary security procedures. The best criteria for determining whether information is exposed is based on whether a competitive advantage is achieved by revealing that information.

Common data is most valuable when appropriately published so that it is useful to your trading partners for the intended purpose. The Web provides a powerful publishing medium. Common-Language is JITCorp's approach to publishing this data in standard formats. Those formats always include a structure usable directly by our business applications as well as other formats typically used in specific industries. There are always nuances in some data that can be difficult to communicate in EDI, XML, or other standard formats.

Currently, fragmented data and application structures separate companies within a supply chain into islands, each speaking its own language and using manual efforts or EDI investments to translate the exact same information needed in exchanges with trading partners. By forming alliances that share industry-common data, these islands can be converted to networks. Figure 3.5 illustrates changing the islands of technology and data into a flow of sales transactions.

Table 3.4 General Data Types: Description, Nature, and Protection Requirements

DATA TYPE	DESCRIPTION	NATURE AND PROTECTION REQUIREMENTS
Proprietary	Intellectual property	Nature: Central to the survival of your company. This data defines such critical details as with whom and how you sell, alliances, finances, patents, and copyrights. Knowledge of this information could directly benefit a competitor. Protection: Restricted to inside the company, lenders, and as few others as is practical.
Transactional	Exchanges with partners	Nature: Contracts and other private details of transactions with each trading partner. Knowledge of this information could directly benefit a competitor. Knowledge outside the participants of a specific transaction could damage relationships with other trading partners. Protection: Protected with contract clauses, nondisclosure agreements.
Common	General industry data	Nature: General, regional, relationship based on publicly or semipublicly released information. This information may be sensitive in nature but in the judgment of the company there is more benefit from some level of public release than there is from keeping it private. Protection: The emphasis shifts from protecting this data to deciding how broadly it should be published.

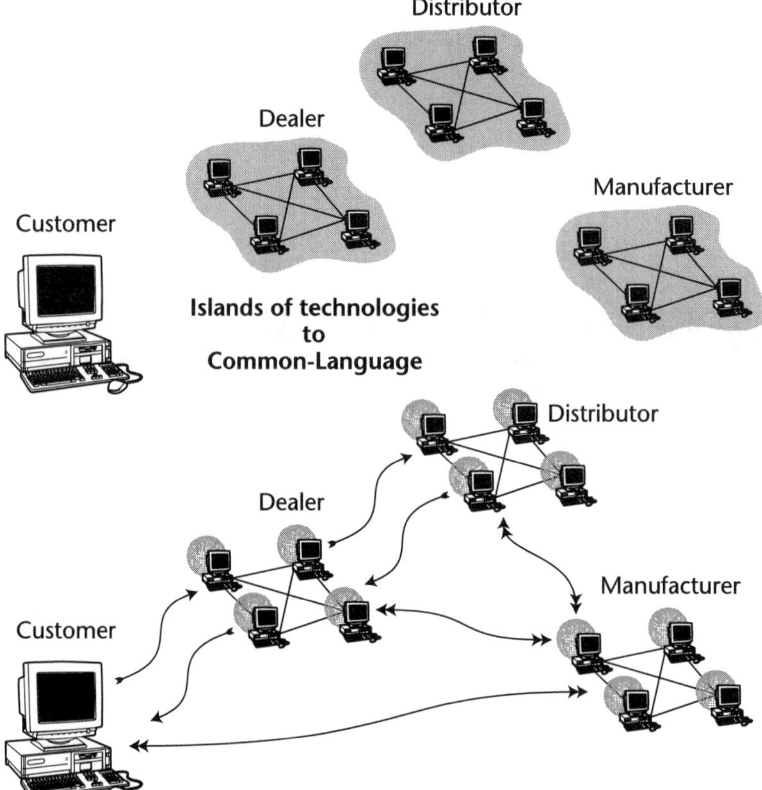

Figure 3.5 Convert islands into sales flow.

Translation Options

Transacting between trading partners is essential. The following is a summary of techniques to manage the details of those transactions:

Electronic Data Interchange (EDI). It is possible to manage relations among trading partners with translation technology. EDI was supposed to manage data complexities by creating standards for data to be transmitted between trading partners. After 30 years of being forced on the market by major buyers, it still has not captured widespread market acceptance.

EDI is a fixed solution in a world of constant flux. It failed to rework all supply chain relationships because it is expensive, difficult to implement, and nearly impossible to maintain. Data constantly changes; formats to communicate data must adapt to these changes. Products, services, and relationships are in constant flux. For the average business this flux is intense; when multiplied by the number of trading partners, it often exceeds available resources.

eXtensible Markup Language (XML). This is a more pliable, Web-based translation technology. It seems, at least initially, that it will be much easier to maintain than EDI. If one part of a translation map changes, it does not cause the entire transaction to fail. It is likely that it will be widely used and will become a strong translation technology.

Common-Language. This approach is better and the tools and techniques in this book will show why. When low-cost and fast speed-to-implement solutions are necessary, using the Common-Language tools allows direct, untranslated transactions to take place among desktops. By eliminating a translation interface, the potential for error is reduced and maintenance of that interface is zero.

Exchanges. Generally these are service companies that manage the exchanges between partners. They can be useful in arranging trades of standard commodities, but most buyers will not accept their use as an added cost to purchase. It seems to be an emotional (not financial) thing, but buyers are very resistant to paying commissions.

Summary

This chapter touched on four key points:

Start with what you know. Build to improve capabilities with existing customers.

Know your required core competencies and competitive requirements. Do not try to change the way human nature has defined business relationships.

Find allies. You share a common problem with a lot of other companies. Look for solutions that share the cost with your trading partners and even competitors. The common-languages provided by companies like Sabre for the travel industry have proved very beneficial to the companies involved.

Learn the tools. Understand enough about how the Web works to use it to make communications an integral aspect of how you do business.

CHAPTER 4

Setting Up a Desktop Hosting Solution

Making choices is difficult when you have little experience. Even committing to small things can cause extensive delays. The hardest part of getting started is beginning. The fear that a wrong choice will be made often prevents action that yields the experience necessary to make correct choices.

Often the first concern I hear when discussing Desktop Hosting is, "What happens if the server goes down?" This question is asked by someone who currently has little ability to interact with customers on the Web. It is like a blind person questioning if they will need glasses when their sight is restored. The answer to unknowns is to start so you get enough experience to make adjustments.

You very likely already have most of the hardware and software required for Desktop Hosting. The changes you'll likely need to make are outlined in this chapter.

Getting Started

The following capabilities and features of Desktop Hosting demonstrate the breadth of application for this concept. These capabilities and features are:

- Relationship and transaction serving
- Little programming required

- Site management
- Search engines
- Catalogs
- Price by customer type
- Web order entry
- Order status
- Shipment tracking
- Proposal status
- Account status
- Service requests
- Email
- Forums and libraries
- FAQ, support, and other features

The general approach to software and hardware that I take in this book is to keep it inexpensive. Once you gain experience, you can adjust based on the specific needs of your communications.

A second aspect of affordability is that many small units can combine into a powerful whole. Many cheap computers ganged together can create a massive processing capability. If one computer out of a group of 10 fails, you have reduced capacity, not a system failure. You can add or trim capacity incrementally with changing demand. This works well on the Web because of its basic approach to resources—Uniform Resource Locators (URLs). A URL defines a path to a resource. You are familiar with it being someone's Web site. It can be very much more. At the end of the path a developer can control what happens next. You can spread a task across multiple computers, multiple locations, serve Web pages, and perform many more tasks. My approach to hardware and software is:

- Inexpensive solutions allow you to get started so that you can gain the experience necessary to adapt to your specific needs.
- Parallel processing by inexpensive solutions is durable and scalable.

Hardware Requirements

Hardware is readily available. Hardware manufacturers have done an excellent job of driving performance and reliability up and costs down. Nearly any new machine today is a viable Web server, and many older machines will operate with the tools provided with this book.

Desktop Computer

The miminum requirements to use the software are:

CPU	200 megahertz or faster
Hard drive	200 megabytes or larger
RAM	128 megabytes or more recommended
CD Drive	To view training movies

Web Servers

The minimum requirements for computers to be interactive Web servers and internal business machines are fairly trivial. Essentially any computer you buy new today for more than $400 is adequate if you install at least 64 megabytes of RAM. Depending on workload, retired machines can be used as servers. General specifications are:

- Hard drive with at least 100 megabytes of free space
- RAM of at least 64 megabytes (more is better, and remarkably cheap)
- Speed of at least 200 megahertz

Security

The Web can be safely servered and transactions managed with your trading partners. If you allow attachments to your email or can receive email on your computer, you are as exposed as you will be when installing a server.

There are typically two points of real risk when opening a server to the Web: the Web serving software and the computer's operating system (with extensions). Specifically:

Web server exposure. Nearly any application could be a Web server. Many programs automatically communicate on the Web. An example is when you receive an alert that there is an update for a software program you have on your machine. The program is most likely exchanging information via the Web. If you install one of several programs like "ZoneAlert" you can see these exchanges. Programs that are "http," "ftp," and "mail" servers extend this capability to allow you much more power. With power comes responsibility.

Most applications that declare they are Web servers have a root directory which limits outside access to a specific folder and any enclosed folders. As you set up a Web server, make sure that this folder is correctly pointed and does not contain information you do not want exposed. WebClerk further limits this folder to being in the same folder as the WebClerk application

Web servers can also set access levels or allow users to access specific directories or resources. Make sure you check these aspects and tighten security parameters to restrict access to the lowest level of the directory that permits the desired interactions.

Operating system exposure. These can be set by you, by applications, or by a virus that exposes your entire machine to intrusion. You need to be aware of the risks, and you should take steps to minimize them.

In addition to the better-known virus risk, there is a third possible area of risk to all machines operated by people. When browsing the Web or reading email attachments, you are sometimes asked to acknowledge a download or accept or cancel an action. Any of these events can be used to install a *starfish.* As a starfish inserts its stomach into a small hole of its prey to digest it; this device inserts a small Web server and search engine that finds interesting files on your computer and posts them out. It can also be used to invite in secondary viruses, worms, and so forth.

Protection from intrusion is manageable. Check with your service and equipment providers. There are also sites that offer security checking features, such as:

- www.anti-virus.com has an Internet-based virus scanner named "HouseCall" that checks your machine for intrusions.
- www.shavic.com, a tool to evaluate NT workstations.
- www.zonealarm.com has a program named "ZoneAlarm" that monitors and controls the capability of programs to use the Internet.

Mix the operating systems of the computers on your network. A virus or attack on one operating system may have no effect on another. We saw this in a number of instances. CodeRed attacks affected Windows computers but had virtually no impact on Macintosh computers. It is my understanding that the Homeland Defense's policy is to mix their networks between Windows, Macs, and Unix operating systems to reduce risk from a single point of attack. We mix our network at about one third Macs. It is my personal belief that the overwhelming dependence on the Windows operating system exposes business to the computer equivalent of the Irish Potato Famine.

Uninterruptable Power Supply

An uninterruptible power supply (UPS) is an important piece of equipment for local Web serving. Like your fax machine, the most likely cause of failure for locally hosted Web servers is electrical or telephone failure caused by storms. These battery units provide stable power neutralizing most fluctuations.

Internet Connection

You will need a connection between your computer and the Web. If your business is not already Web-enabled, you will need to find an Internet service provider. Depending on the connection option, you may need to acquire a modem/router (could be separate or combined). Although it is possible to buy this directly, my recommendation is buy it from your provider. If there is a problem or just confusion, a single point of responsibility will easily pay for itself in peace of mind.

Table 4.1 shows the various hosting options available. Desktop Hosting can be deployed in combination with your existing Web site, particularly as you develop and test your new, interactive, unattended communications solution.

Table 4.1 Hosting Options to Optimize Communication Efforts

OPTION	STRENGTHS	LIABILITIES
Desktop Hosting	Directly linked to the data and relationships being served. Control of data. Locally maintained. Local marketing capabilities.	Locally maintained. Bandwidth must match demand.
Remote hosting	Professionally serviced. Large bandwidth. Excellent bandwidth and storage of movies, graphics and other large files that would slow down your interactive site.	Remote from the source. Data synchronization is complex.
Application service provider (ASP)	Professionally serviced. Typically reliable hardware.	Vendor profitability unproven. May or may not be interactive with your data. Data synchronization is complex.
Mall, a variation on ASP (example, Yahoo stores)	Easy setup. Professionally maintained. Marketing resources.	You give away customer list and their buying patterns.

Software

A very wide variety of software can be used to create Desktop Hosting servers. (see Figure 4.1). The important issue is to look at how work is being done at your company and make the application and server communicate that data interactively. As data is changed to meet internal needs, its relevant aspects must be published to the correct Web users.

Various software components combine to manage interactive Web sites. (See Figure 4.1.) To the left of each block is an example software program that can be used to manage functions of the block. There are many other programs that can be used in place of those listed. WebClerk is provided on the CD included with this book. It combines several components to simplify implementations.

WebClerk is an integrated database, application, and Web server.

Database

The database software shown in Figure 4.1 has two components:

Data. This is the actual data. It is stored in SQL or the format accessible by the data engine.

Data engine. This can be Oracle, MySQL, Microsoft SQLServer, 4D, or others. The choice can be made based on the best combination of capabilities and cost.

Application

The application software shown in Figure 4.1 has two components:

Engine interface. Most applications have an integrated interface to the data engine. A special interface is beneficial if you wish to use the same application with various data engines. You can avoid using the built-in interface and write your own for each combination you need. For example, for a single-user situation, it may be beneficial to use MySQL, and in large client/server situations to use Oracle. The engine interface allows you to use the same application for both cases.

Application. This is the business logic program.

Web and Applet Server

The Web and applet server receives Web addresses (URLs) and passes them to the application (if the request is for dynamic resources) or serves the static resources. Applets are small programs that get sent to a user's browser for added capabilities.

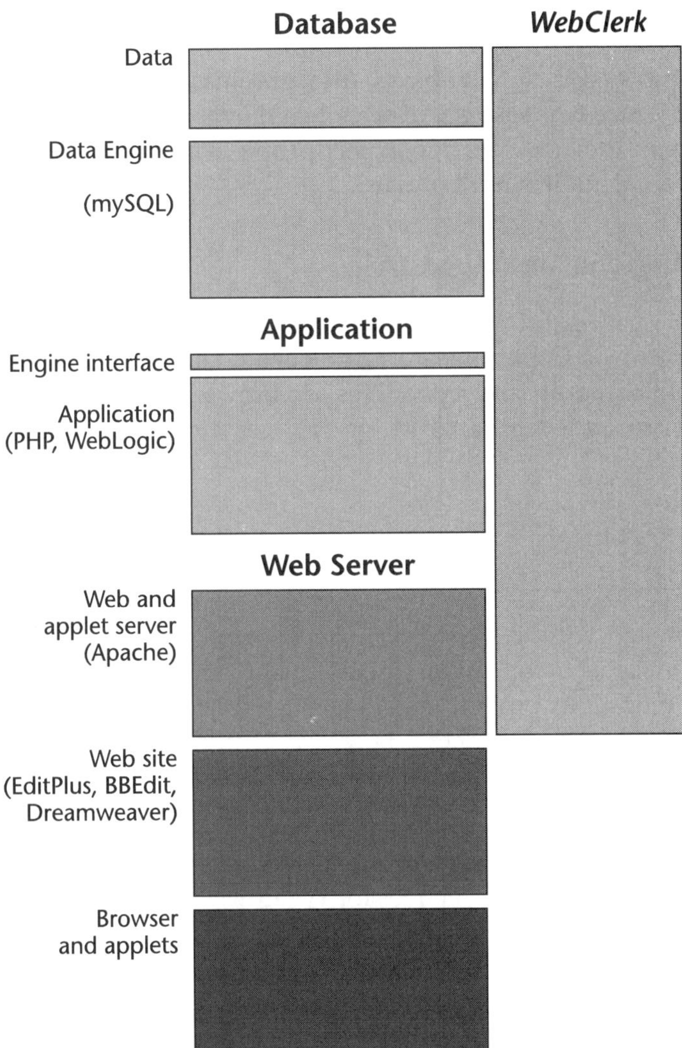

Figure 4.1 Software components in an interactive Web site.

Resources require specific handling to be useful to the user's browser. They are declared with a MIME designation by the server when being sent to the user's browser. These resources may also require plug-ins to be useful to the user. Make sure that if you are using resources that require plug-ins, you also provide a means for the user to obtain the plug-in. Examples of such resources are QuickTime movies, Flash, AVI, and so on.

Web Site

The Web site is the collection of objects, files, graphics, and templates for data resources that house what users will see when they look at the site. Be sure to test your sites on the browsers you expect people will use to view your site; HTML is common, but it is not standard.

Browsers, Plug-Ins, and Applets

Browsers are client-side display programs, typically Microsoft Internet Explorer or Netscape Communicator. Applets are small programs sent by a server to add to or modify the capabilities of a browser while a user is at your site. Plug-ins are added capabilities of browsers to handle these specific resources.

Examples CD

The CD distributed with this book contains examples built using WebClerk, which is an affordable tool that you can use to implement an interactive, unattended communications project. Installing the application will install all the software, data, and Web components necessary to implement a Desktop Hosting solution. The items that get installed are shown in Figure 4.2 and are explained here:

- The jitWeb folder contains prefabricated Web pages and images. The jitWebCE folder contains pages for Window CE devices.
- Mac4DX and Win4DX folders contain extensions to the WebClerk application.
- ASIFont.fon, ASINIPPC.dll, ASIPORT.RSR, PROC.ESR, and QTDP32.dll must remain in the same folder as the WebClerk application.
- ASIFont.map can be used to change the fonts used by WebClerk between Windows and Macintosh computers. The key font in this map is the Geneva to Tahoma conversion. If your machine does not have Tahoma, you may have to change this font map.
- WebClerkXXp.4DD and WebClerkXXp.4DR are the data file and the data resources. XX is 9 in this image. It may change depending on the version of the program on your disk. On the Macintosh these two files are combined, and the filename ends in .data.
- WebClerkXX.4DC, WebClerkXX.EXE, and WebClerkXX.RSR are the components of the WebClerk application. On the Macintosh, these components are a single file.

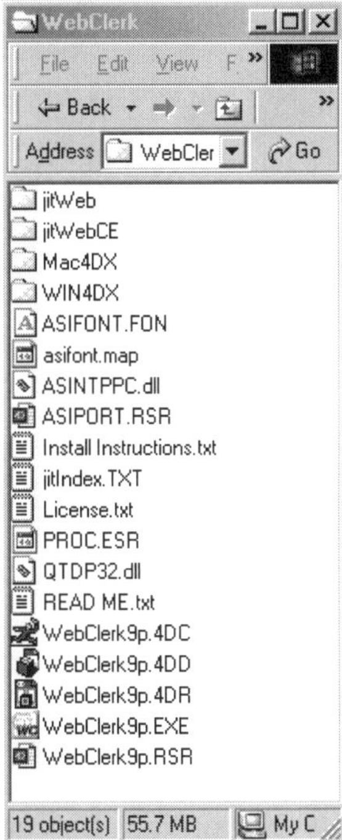

Figure 4.2 List of key files in the WebClerk folder.

JITWeb Folder

The jitWeb folder on the CD contains the Web pages, images, movies, Flash, and other MIME types to be displayed from the local host. Pages can be simple HTML or they can have comprehensive JavaScript, applets, and other features. To simplify Desktop Hosting, all critical tasks are managed on the server side. This also improves security because only the commands deemed acceptable can be called. These commands can be tightly limited so that the level of technical expertise required is reduced.

There are three basic types of pages, which are outlined in Figure 4.3:

- Search pages from which searches are executed (...Srch.html)
- List pages that return lists of records matching search criteria (...List.html)
- Record pages that return a record when only one record matches a search criteria (...Rec.html)

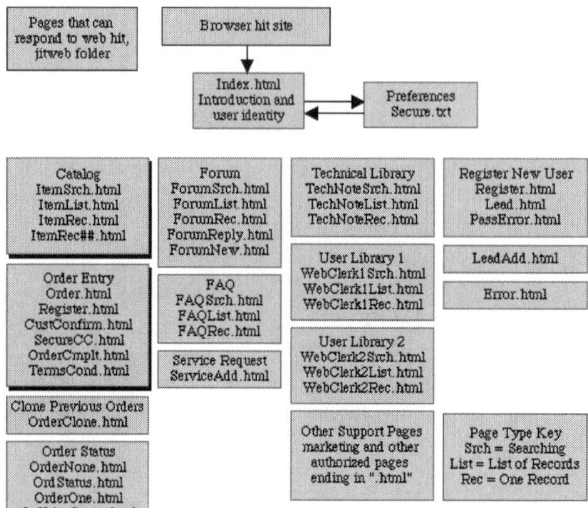

Figure 4.3 Prefabricated pages.

Figure 4.4 illustrates the search logic. There are several options for controlling the pages that display the results of searches. Figure 4.5 shows templates. They have database references on them that are converted to values as the pages are served by the server.

The value of !jit= declares to the server that there is a value to be evaluated and converted. As an example, the second aspect, 2, declares that the value should come from the Table 2 or [Customers] table in WebClerk. The third value, 81, declares that the value of the 81st field or email should be displayed. The ! ends the instruction. When the server sends this page (shown in Figure 4.6), these values are converted into the actual values in the database record.

Data flows through the page templates to display values and accept values from forms back into the database (see Figure 4.7). Getting used to pointing at values in the database is probably one of the more complex aspects of implementing integrated physical and Web commercial solutions. It is very much simplified when you understand that the Web pages in your site are templates. As the database/Web server delivers these pages to a viewer, the data reference tags (!jit=2;4!) are replaced by the value of the fields in the database.

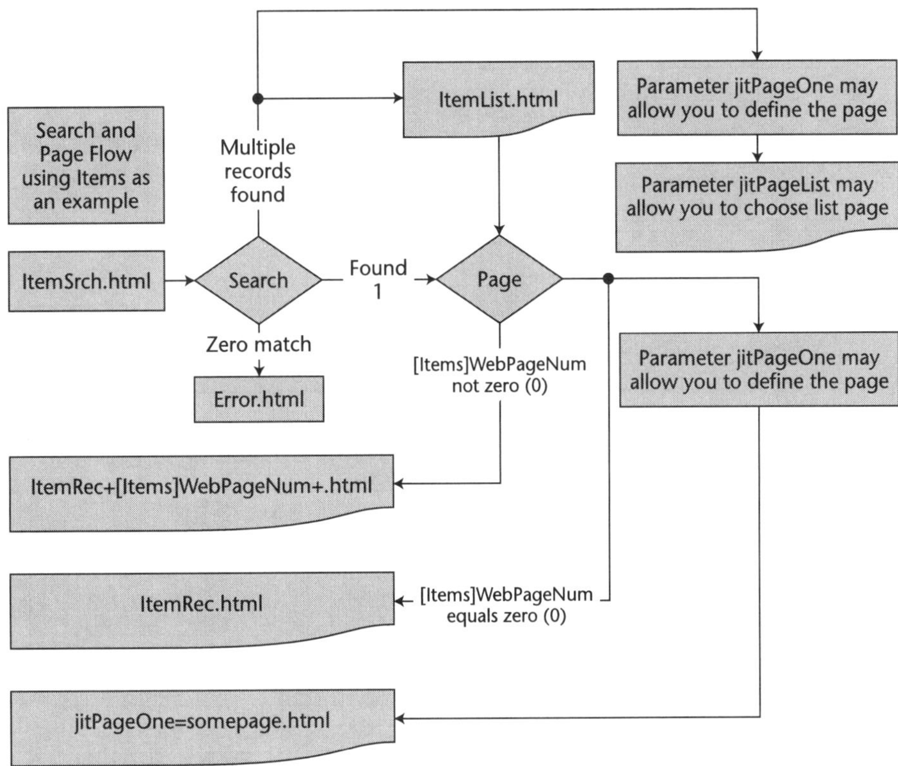

Figure 4.4 Search logic.

Email1	!jit=2;81!	
Company:	!jit=2;2!	
Name First/Last:	!jit=2;73!	!jit=2;23!

Figure 4.5 Page template before displaying to the Web.

Email1	bill@jitcorp.com	
Company:	James Integrated Technologies	
Name First/Last:	Terra	James

Figure 4.6 Page Template as displayed to the Web.

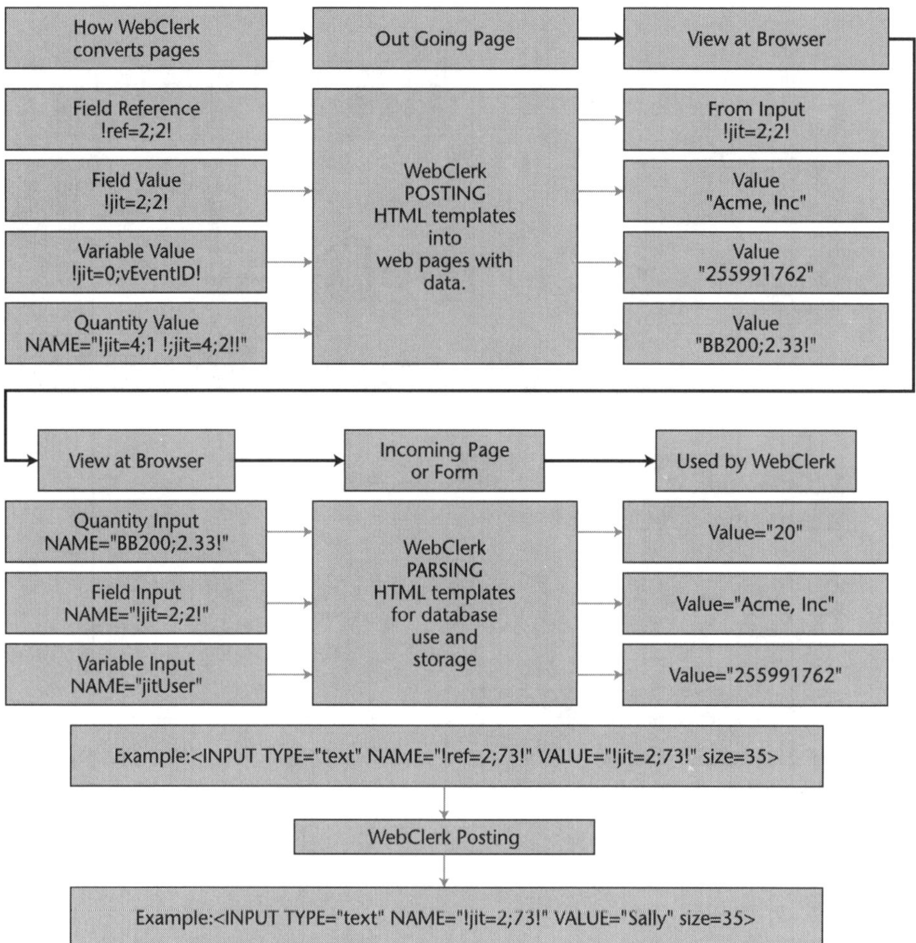

Figure 4.7 Data flow values.

Client/Server and Web Servers

The power of individual Web servers can be integrated into comprehensive client/server implementations. Figure 4.8 illustrates adding Web serving to the desktops of the many people who must accomplish specific tasks within your organization. Integrating the data that changes as people do their jobs and customer communications are key aspects of Desktop Hosting. They change unattended communications from "Leave a message" to "Here's your answer."

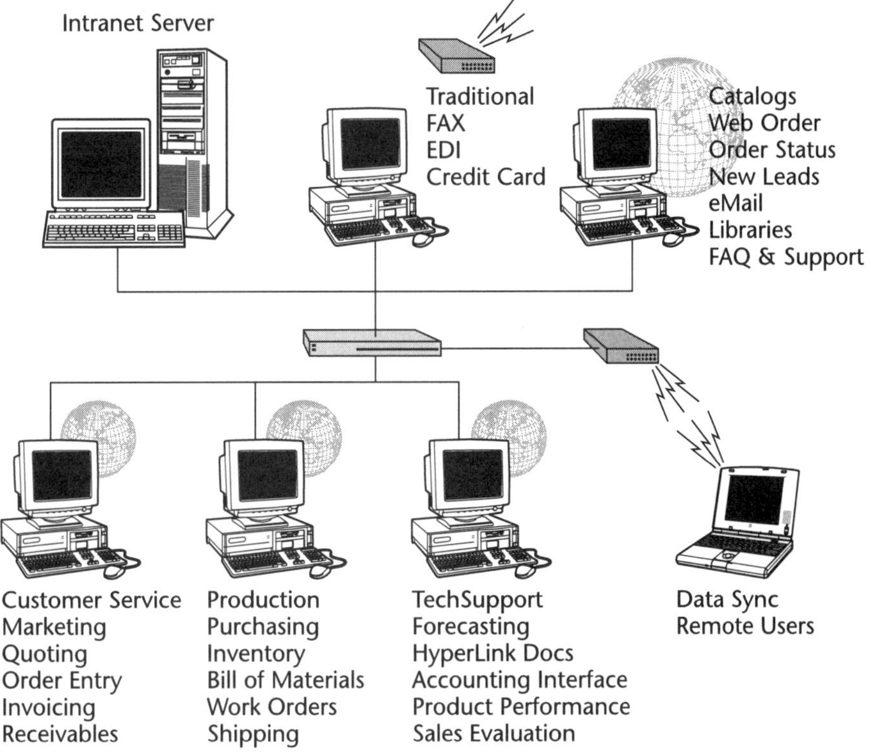

Figure 4.8 Client/Server and Web serving integrated at the desktop.

Summary

Many additional examples, case studies, documents, and coding samples are on the CD that is distributed with this book and on the Web sites www. Webclerk.com and www.DesktopHosting.com. Major points to remember are:

- The hardware required for Desktop Hosting is readily available.
- Desktop Hosting can be managed in single-user or in a comprehensive client/server system.
- The tools that let you gain experience are available on the CD.

PART TWO

How Desktop Hosting Works

CHAPTER 5

Getting a Project Funded, Keeping It Funded

The best way to get and keep a project funded is to get your entire staff involved and overwhelm them with the value that their involvement returns. This is the "small bites, lots of friends" approach to making changing an organization. In this chapter we look at how to get buy-in from different groups in your company and how to make the return on investment overwhelm the cost and fear of making changes.

Desktop Hosting, putting the point of communications at the point of action, involves everyone in your company. It spreads the effort across your entire team. The sense of winning and that you will continue to win grows across your entire company. Spreading the value, spreading the wealth, getting a tangible return for everyone involved is the best way to get a projected funded and to keep it funded.

What Is in It for Me?

Getting buy-in requires that people understand how they personally will benefit and how their group will benefit. It requires that people accept that the benefits are worth the pain they will have to go through to change their ways. This return on pain (ROP) is a critical aspect of driving change in an organization.

A real problem with the effects of change is that the pain is immediate and the benefit happens some time later. Making the benefit happen at the same time as the change, keeping your objectives achievable, and breaking the tasks into actions that can be accomplished in a couple of hours can speed acceptance. Several items are included with this book to help you effect the positive changes of moving to Desktop Hosting:

- There are 150 movies on the CD that comes with the book. They walk through features and techniques.
- QuickStart and Learning Exercises on the CD contain step-by-step exercises.
- The Web sites at www.WebClerk.com and www.DesktopHosting.com provide forums and additional information and exercises.
- Case studies in Chapter 7 illustrate specific benefits for specific groups in your company:

Sales. Case Studies 1, 2, and 3 demonstrate how to make the Web a sales tool. Specific exercises are listed that show customers' their account balances and order status. A script illustrates using the Web to make more sales calls; more sales calls relate directly to more commissions.

Customer service. Case Studies 1, 4, and 5 illustrate service requests, order status, and shipping records.

Marketing. Case Studies 2, 3, 4, and 6 show the advantages of published-based versus message-based communications and how Desktop Hosting can be configured to enhance relationships between your company and your customers.

Purchasing. Case Studies 6 and 7 provide examples of how increasing profitable sales results from giving buyers Web tools to control the cost of goods.

Engineering, manufacturing, and production. Case Studies 2, 3, 4, and 7 show how publishing specifications, quality control documents, ISO 9000 documentation, and supply chain automation benefit those responsible for adding value at the lowest practical cost.

Information technology. All case studies show how technology can be applied to simplify the selling process.

Management. Case Studies 6 and 7 break the expensive aspects of implementing technology into affordable and achievable pieces.

Educators. Case Study 8 provides exercises for students and is intended to bridge the interest of business, students, and educators.

Overview of Implementation

After you familiarize yourself with this chapter, read the case studies in Chapter 7. Then come back to this chapter and think about how to achieve a successful implementation in your company. As a part of the implementation process, do the step-by-step exercises with the software and demo data provided with this book. When you are ready, follow these top-level steps:

1. Walk departments through these exercises to illustrate how they can reach an achievable result for a small commitment.
2. Write up your plan (or plans if you have multiple profit centers).
3. Execute your Desktop Hosting solution to enhance your communications and increase the value associated with expanding relationships with your trading partners.

Plan for Implementing Desktop Hosting

Break Desktop Hosting into bite-size pieces. Draft plans for profit centers within your company. Align the specific responsibilities in these plans with the self-interests of groups in your company. The plans provided in this book follow a specific format that adds clarity to operating in a competitive environment where not all facts and consequences are known. It is designed to clearly and efficiently keep many independent operating units united under a common objective. The components are:

Objective. A one-sentence statement of who, what, why, when, and where.

Background. Describes the general situation, things that help, things that hinder.

Execution. Describes the details of how the plan will be effected.

Finance and Logistics. Contains detail on resources allocation.

Communications. Shares information to coordinate, command, and control.

Note that communications is an integral part of the operations plan, not a separate task. This powerful tool for unattended communications—Desktop Hosting—needs to remain an integral part of the plans for your company. As time passes, you will see how to become even more effective with your implementation. Communications is the aspect of leadership that distributes a clear understanding of how everyone profits from his or her relationship with your company.

The Plan Format

Implement a plan with the intent to increase profitable sales.

Objective: Who, What, Why, When, and Where

The objective statement is a single sentence that describes:

Who: Your company

What: Make use of the Web for 40 sales and service calls and take 15 orders via the Web from existing customers

Where: Within their existing markets

When: Within one month of the initial effort

Why: To expand competitiveness and service and cut communications costs

Background Section

The background section describes the general situation: things that help and things that hinder progress on the plan. It typically describes:

- Who is on the team—name/phone/email address/URL for the following contacts: approval, administrative, data, training, accounting, and outside support.
- Top priorities listed in order of importance. Execution will be managed in accordance with priorities. Be specific and narrow. Once you build a pattern of success, you can broaden it. Biting off more than can be chewed will result in failure by design.
- The current system, including a summary of good points, bad points, current connection to the Internet, required Internet load, current concerns, and work-arounds that might affect the plan, and a list of five key customers, vendors, and outside advisors to review the site for form and function.

Execution (How)

The execution section describes details of *how* the plan will be effected.

Concept

The concept is to change the standard for unattended communication from message- to publish-based by integrating internal data and activities with Web-based communications.

Keep the effort focused on narrow, specifically defined, and achievable tasks. Avoid trying to manage every exception and unusual case encountered until sufficient experience has been developed to evaluate its importance and reasonable and affordable options for incorporating them are known.

Keep costs affordable so that adjustments can be made based on successes and failures.

Specific Responsibilities

Tailoring your sites to your specific needs requires entering details about your customers, products, and general business practices into the database and the design of the Web interface. You can use the demo data to do much of the training. You can also use the demo data as a base to build your own interactive data set. Table 5.1 provides a checklist of tasks that you should perform.

There are conversion mechanisms to convert data from existing systems and for importing it into the program. In many companies, a great many of the nuances of how to do business are in peoples' heads. Assembling the details is generally one of the largest tasks in getting a computer system to be truly interactive. Table 5.2 breaks the typical tasks into small sections so that the effort can be realistically estimated. There are very likely other tasks that would be beneficial to add to this list for your company.

Table 5.1 Specific Tasks

DATE (DAYS)	TASK	STATUS
Day 1	Read book	
Day 1	Install WebClerk	
Day 2	Take orders, service customers, and purchase on the Web	
Days 2-20	Complete Learning Exercises to achieve incremental success	
Day 3-30	Modify sites to meet needs	
Day 3-30	Build experience	
Day 30+	Open exchanges with trading partners	

Table 5.2 Detailed Activity List

SETUP	WHO	BUDGET	ACTUAL	EXPECTED	COMPLETED
Loading software					
Set up for multiuser use					
Data conversion/setup:					
	Accounts				
	Bills of material				
	Carriers				
	Customers/mfgrs.				
	Contacts				
	Defaults				
	Employees				
	Invoices/receivables				
	Items				
	Jobs				
	Leads				
	Letters				
	Orders				
	Orders comments				
	Passwords				
	Payments/credits				
	Pop-ups				
	Process/causes				
	Proposals				
	Purchase orders				
	Report structures				
	Reps				
	Scripts				
	Sources				
	Special discounts				
	Tax jurisdictions				
	Terms				
	Territories				
	Usage				
	Other ________				
	Other ________				

SETUP	WHO	BUDGET	ACTUAL	EXPECTED	COMPLETED
Data management					
Administration					
	Form/report design				
	Data synchronization				
	Import/export				
	Passwords				
	Process commissions				
	Tally				
	Accounting interface				
Inventory management					
	Place/receive PO's				
	Adjust inventory/ BOM's				
	Forecast needs				
Order processing skills					
	Enter orders/invoices				
	Convert orders to invoices Change terms/ reps				
	Change tax jurisdiction				
	Carriers/shipping				
	Change line details				
	Forms selection				
	List inventory status & specs				
	Track status and actions				
Printing					
	Forms properly print				
	Primary forms selected				

(continues)

Table 5.2 Detailed Activity List (Continued)

SETUP	WHO	BUDGET	ACTUAL	EXPECTED	COMPLETED
Sales management					
	Organize calls by calendar				
	Forecast sales				
	Review marketing performance				
	Collect receivables				
	Customer service				
Web site design					
	Related sites				
	Graphical interface				
	Speed issues				
	Load Issues				
	Bandwidth				
	Defaults				
	IP address				
	Secure credit card				
	Security				
	Passwords				
	ftp				
Features					
	Enter orders				
	Clone orders				
	Proposal status				
	Order status				
	Shipping status				
	Catalogs				
	Specials				
	Sign-in				
	Registration				
	TechNotes				
	Libraries				
	FAQ				

SETUP	WHO	BUDGET	ACTUAL	EXPECTED	COMPLETED
	Forums				
	Service requests				
	eMail				
	Other pages and features				
Customer response					
	Registration email				
	Order email				
	email response PO				
	Mapping to customer PO system				

Logistics and Finance

Allocate the funds and resources to implement the tasks. Nothing will demoralize a team or cause failure faster than defining achievable objectives while allocating insufficient resources to achieve them. The hardware required to implement this plan is available in most companies today. A connection to the Internet can quickly pay for itself. Communications resources and support for Desktop Hosting are provided from four sources:

1. Written instructions contained in this book; there is also extensive interactive documentation provided with the WebClerk application on the CD.
2. Movies provided with the training CD.
3. Interactive forums at www.webclerk.com and www.desktophosting.com for the included programs and for the Desktop Hosting industry in general.
4. Purchasable support from your choice of vendors.

Summary

I often hear people say things like, "We are in a backward industry" or "Our customers are not technical" or "Our people lack the skills needed." If you need to communicate to compete, give your people and your trading partners tools to win. Simplify the technical aspects, provide the communications, get experience, and then adjust. You will never hit the target if you never pull the trigger. The hardest part about getting started is beginning.

At one time, it was technically difficult to network computers within a company. Transferring files required copying them on to floppies and sneaker-netting them to the desired machine. Today, nearly every company is internally networked, and yet we sneaker-net between our internal network and the external networks required to communicate with our trading partners. If you show the concepts in this book to your trading partners, by the time you finish the training exercises you will have an interactive network among your employees, customers, and vendors.

> *...the prime law of networks: value explodes exponentially with membership, while this value explosion sucks in yet more members.*
>
> Kevin Kelly—"New Rules for the New Economy," *Wired* magazine, September 1997

As described by Kevin Kelly, networks explode in value as members are added. Add your vendors and your customers to yours. Your company can be ahead of or behind this change depending on your leadership, your ability to communicate, and your ability to rally diverse interests to a common purpose. The competitive consequences of this are real. I did not make up this "law"; I simply emphasize it while giving you the tools to secure an advantage for your company. The 1997 magazine article was expanded into a book by Kevin Kelly, *New Rules for the New Economy (1998)*. For further background, I suggest you read this book because it is very insightful and forward-looking; also read Hagel and Armstrong's *Net Gain* (1997).

Communications is an aspect of leadership. It focuses the diverse interests of your people and the people you do business with into action to achieve a common purpose: to profit, to add more value than the cost to compete.

CHAPTER 6

How to Manage and Adapt

The tools that can be used to manage the Web grow more powerful all the time, and, generally, they also grow easier to use. You will be surprised at how much you learn, and how quickly, as you begin to take the actions described in this book. Refer to this chapter during the implementation, deployment, and tuning of your Desktop Hosting sites.

Simplify

It may seem paradoxical, but as the amount of information on the Internet and the Web has grown, it has actually become easier to access, use, and publish this data. It gets easier as those who understand the meaning of the information control the tools for publishing to the Web. It gets easier when the constantly changing data that supports business transactions is automatically published. Desktop Hosting offers further significant advances in this simplification process. Here are some examples of how it does this.

Relevant Content

Serving your Web site from your desktop integrates real-time data that is of direct interest to your Web visitor (customers and vendors).

User-Created Content

Your company becomes the host for common interests of your customers. Integrating forums into your site allows your trading partners to exchange ideas in a process that you host. You become the meeting room in which unpaid experts in your field exchange ideas, thereby increasing the importance and value of your site for your customers.

Prefabricated Web Sites

Key pages are built into the site provided with this book. Also provided is the software to run and host it, driving down the number of thing you are required to create from scratch. The pages for this site are stored in the jitWeb folder, which you will find in the same folder as the WebClerk application on the accompanying CD.

The pages are templates. As the WebClerk server delivers them, the templates replace data objects with the available records from the database. These pages can contain fixed text, graphics, data objects, database objects, and page objects. Templates and objects reduce the amount of Web site development required.

Site Editor

The Site Editor is located in WebClerk and can be accessed from the Admin Dept >> WebClerk menu of the WebClerk application or from the WebClerk Flow layout. It provides a way to view the pages in the site, make database-managed changes to the site, and open the pages in the desired application for specific HTML editing.

Pages are displayed in the Site Editor in list format, as shown in Figure 6.1. Across the top of the Edit Web Page screen are buttons that act on any pages that have been highlighted and selected from the list displayed. A minor editing capability is also provided just above the list of pages to make small changes to the selected pages. This is a limited editing tool. The primary method for editing these pages is any standard HTML editing program. I personally use BBEdit and Macromedia Dreamweaver on a Mac, and EditPlus and Dreamweaver on a Windows-based PC.

Editing Details

This section has some very detailed information on using the Site Editor. It is included here to further explain Figure 6.1 and so that you may gain an understanding of how data is extracted from database fields and projected into HTML-based template pages.

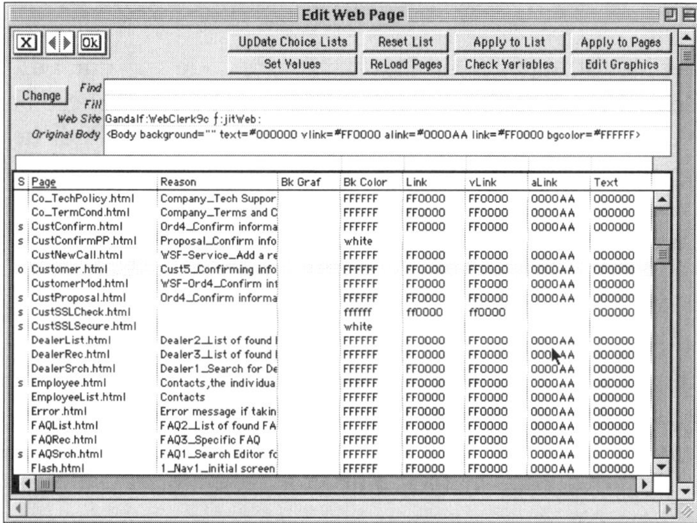

Figure 6.1 The Site Editor lists pages located in the jitWeb folder.

Access to pages in the primary editing program is supported by double-clicking on the page you want to see. The first time you do this you set up your application Helper for HTML documents. You can change your WebClerk Helper application in the Script Editor. Double-clicking on a page will display the page in the HTML editor of your choice.

Database Objects

The S column notes if there are Select lists (s), Objects (o), or both (b) on pages. These identify pages that have database objects. For example, the Customer.html page has an o signifying an object. This object is a list of product categories as defined in the unique values of published records from the [Items]TypeID field. Highlight this page in the Site Editor and click on the Update Choice Lists button to rebuild the list of choices. View the source code for this page and you will see the database object:

```
<!--jitObject=4;items;itemtype;-->
<TABLE><TR><TD vALIGN="top"ALIGN="Center"><BR><A HREF="/item_List?item-
Type=112EGChild&*jitUser=!jit=0;vlEventID!*" TARGET="Main_Frame"><FONT
FACE="Arial" SIZE="2">112EGChild</FONT></A>
<BR><A HREF="/item_List?itemType=113MDStock&*jitUser=!jit=0;vlEventID!*"
TARGET="Main_Frame"><FONT FACE="Arial" SIZE="2">113MDStock</FONT></A>
...
<!--jitObjectEnd-->
```

Data Objects

Open the Customer.html page. Look at the source code and you will see data objects in the form of !jit=2;2!, !jit=0;vlEventID!, and others. These objects are converted to data as the page is displayed to a Web visitor, and they can be checked using the Site Editor. Click on a page to be checked, then click the Check Variables button. The data objects on that page are evaluated and the value, error, or uncertainty will be listed for the page.

Script Editor

A Script Editor is provided to help manage Helper applications, template pages, and data objects. The Script Editor, shown in Figure 6.2, can be accessed from the File menu >> Script Editor or from the WebClerk Flow layout. It is used to generate HTML code that has embedded references to database fields.

By choosing a table and fields, various HTML features can be drafted from within WebClerk. Once drafted, the feature can be pasted into any standard HTML editor. The application Helpers can also be viewed in this window by clicking on the Helpers button. Make desired changes, highlight the desired changes, and then click the Save button.

www.DesktopHosting.com

The Desktop Hosting site will be maintained to keep you informed of other tools that will benefit you in simplifying your Web efforts. You are invited to participate in the online forums at www.desktophosting.com to share your knowledge with and learn insights from others using the same tools.

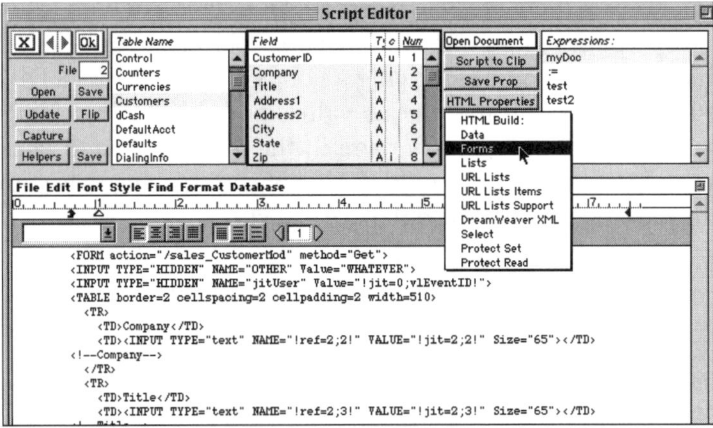

Figure 6.2 The Script Editor.

Complexities

As experience advances and sites evolve, there are many ways of improving the look of the standard site provided in the demo. There are many good books and Web sites about Web site design, but also consider these ideas:

- Introduce better design elements to your Web pages with features from HTML, JavaScript, and Flash.
- Use Dreamweaver, Go-Live, BBEdit, EditPlus, or another Web page editor to enhance your Web pages.
- Choose the colors of your Web site so that they match; integrate the look and feel of your Desktop Hosting site with your brand identity.
- Create graphics, logos, photos, and other elements, but remember that many of your users may have low bandwidth, so keep files sizes small and skip gratuitous "eye candy."
- Use PhotoShop or another graphics program to enhance product views and other elements.
- Learn about advances in telecommunications to optimize your bandwidth. Work with a vendor to drive down costs and maximize the usefulness of your site.
- Data is constantly changing. Keeping a site current and relevant requires it to adjust to the changing data. Make sure your site always reflects the actual state of your business; don't allow your data to decay.

Business, technology, esthetics, communications, human behavior, and other factors combine to make the dot.com world seem more magical than technical. Use that magic to drive your business relationships. Simplify your technology, apply it where it is most useful, and apply it to reinforce the relationships that make your company competitive. Expand your unattended communications so that your relationships are served the information they need when they want it.

Follow Success

Do not let *perfect* be the enemy of *good*. Use the prefabricated elements and demo data provided to build experience. Add your data and graphics, too, so it works in a context you are familiar with. With experience, plan adjustments to ensure that your site always works at its best. In the next chapter, the experiences of several companies that have introduced Desktop Hosting are highlighted.

CHAPTER 7

Case Studies

By now, you should be familiar with the basics of changing unattended communications from message-based to publish-based and of finding practices that work and modifying them to your specific needs. The case studies in this chapter will help you to modify the basic technology. Read through them to get ideas about how to adapt Desktop Hosting to meet the needs of your company. Each one shows how to change the configuration to meet different functional requirements and, taken as a whole, they offer training in how to customize Desktop Hosting. Although the following case studies may be limited in scope, they are specific examples of how the concepts of Desktop Hosting are being applied in actual business situations.

About the Case Studies

The following case studies are presented in this chapter:

Case Study 1 provides an example of extending sales-force capabilities out on to the Web.

Case Study 2 outlines the techniques for products that can be configured. A typical one-page, pizza-ordering sheet has about 30,000 distinct possibilities. Pizza is used as an example of how to manage complex configurations on the Web.

Case Study 3 describes online publishing. This is a mechanism for supporting the publishing and public relations supply chain.

Case Study 4 is a review of how SEGA uses the Web and graphical order entry to manage spare parts sales.

Case Study 5 shows how a small retailer with special shipping needs can use Desktop Hosting.

Case Study 6 uses hotels to demonstrate how to apply Desktop Hosting to support the varied profit centers in a single business.

Case Study 7 discusses Wine Operations, a supply chain automation effort in the wine industry.

Case Study 8 illustrates how schools can use Desktop Hosting to empower their many stakeholders. It is also is an example of how to keep alumni connected over time.

Setup

In all the exercises you will need to operate WebClerk and your browser as follows:

1. Launch WebClerk in its original installation configuration. See QuickStart and Learning Exercises, in the TechNotes window that automatically opens on launch, for more details about managing the various applications and files.
2. In the WebClerk Flow window, launch the WebClerk Server: Click on the fourth button under QuickStart.
3. In the WebClerk Flow window, open the Site Editor (center-bottom button under Resources). The Site Editor window will open, showing the pages in the jitWeb folder; it will be used regularly to look at Web pages to see the interface between the HTML pages and the WebClerk database.
4. Go to your browser. Open a Web page to your local machine as the Web server. This is usually Port 80 and the address of the local machine is http://127.0.0.1. Review the QuickStart and Learning Exercises.

Case Study 1: Increasing Sales Force Capabilities via the Web

The Web is a powerful sales tool. This case study illustrates how to integrate an outside sales force into your unattended communications.

Specification

Objective: Improve the ability to coordinate with customers and a remote sales force.

Point of Interest:

- Increase the impact of physical sales calls with Web presentation.
- Provide remote salespeople with customer status, order status, and the ability to manage call reports from the field.

Concerns: The system needs to be secure so that only authorized people can make modifications to the site. Salespeople need to be selling, and the interface to their information should not impede their productivity.

Lessons:

1. It is practical to manage selling activities and call reports via the Web.
2. When making sales calls, it is beneficial to walk customers through the company Web site.
3. Giving customers their own passwords permits them to see their account balances, order status, recent shipments, and other service and support activities.
4. Selling activities can be managed by giving salespeople the ability to submit call reports from any Web access point.
5. The complexities of selling to a manufacturer, wholesaler, or independent sales representative can be managed within a business application.

Industry: Companies currently using the Web sales force modules include:

- AMJ Equipment, www.amjequipment.com, sells hydraulic systems and components to industrial and municipal customers. Operational aspects include manufacturing, distribution, and sales representation.
- Marin Mountain Bike, www.marinbikes.com, manufactures and sells bicycles. Its customers are retail bike stores.
- Stohlquist Water Wear, www.stohlquist.com, manufactures and sells cold water protective clothing and equipment. Customers are retail sporting goods stores.

User comment:

It is great to be able to show our sales reps more detail than we would show retail customers visiting our site. It is even better that our reps can know what is in stock and sell what is available, not just what is possible.

Bonnie Stohlquist—Stohlquist Water Wear

Pricing: Pricing has to support different tiers of buyers: items may be sold to a distributor or to an independent sales representative, with different pricing for each buyer. Commission tracking is tied to the marginal profit of products sold by each buyer.

General Needs: Manage internal and external sales, inventory, and installation. Manage customer relations.

Security: Accounts are paid for by check. No special effort is required. Secure sign-in is an option.

Hardware: The intranet uses a standard 10/100 10BaseT network with typical computers. It is a multiplatform environment with both Windows and Macintosh operating systems.

Software:

- Intranet is provided by a CommerceExpert client/server configuration.
- Extranet WebClerk servers are clients to the intranet CommerceExpert server. WebSalesForce is a separate feature that supports field sales force automation.

Features: Manage manufacturing company sales.

Sign-in: Reps and employees can sign in with different authority than customers. When they sign in, they are given a screen that shows their open activities and the records of their customers.

Learning Exercises

When working through this example, you will act as a remote sales person:

1. Sign in to the database.
2. Look up current activity.
3. Check open orders, work orders, and proposals for which you are responsible.
4. Review a list of customers and leads that have active follow-up requirements.
5. Find a specific customer.
6. Help a customer see the status of any orders.
7. Conduct a sales presentation to a customer using the Web.

NOTE

These steps are based on using the single-user WebClerk demo as it is supplied on the CD accompanying this book. If you have taken actions that will prevent you from having access to the data and features in the demo data, install a new copy and work from the original setup to assure all the components of data, Web pages, and procedures are available.

The client/server configuration has the WebSalesForce features available as a separate module, and a key must be purchased to enable these features.

It is a good idea to look at Appendix A (on the CD) to see the flow charts associated with WebSalesForce.

Sign in to the Database

1. Sign in with the username Employee and password test. A Web page will display the Employee.html page showing the [Employees] record information and a query engine to look for specific records (Figure 7.1). When the page is submitted, the `Search_User` command is executed.

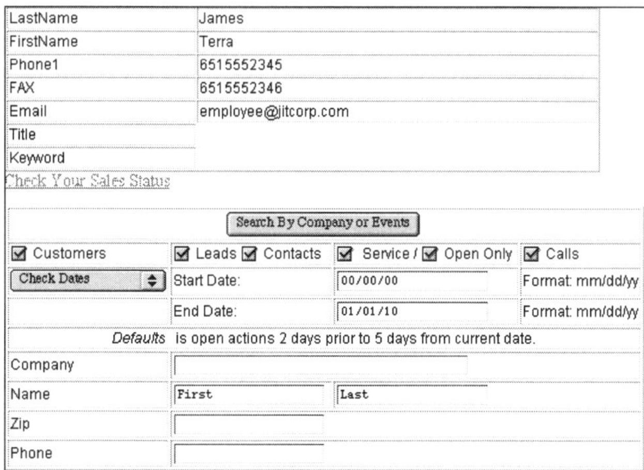

Figure 7.1 Web page Employee.html.

NOTE

Web sign-in is *not* case sensitive (too many users forget the Caps Lock key). You can increase security by having the sign-in page transmitted within an SSL-secured connection. That way the username and password are not passed in the clear.

2. SSL Security may be added to WebClerk (see www.WebClerk.com for specifics) and changing the call to the sign-in page on the Index_NavBar.html page. Change the link from:

   ```
   <A href="/SignIn.html*jitUser=!jit=0;vlEventID!*" target="Main_Frame">
   ```

   to:

   ```
   <A
   href="https://AddressForYourMachine/SignIn.html*jitUser=!jit=0;vlEven-
   tID!*" target="Main_Frame">
   ```

NOTE

AddressForYourMachine is the DNS name for your computer or the TCP/IP address of your computer.

3. From the WebClerk Site Editor view the Index_NavBar.html and Signin.html pages in your preferred HTML editing program. Note the form command and variables on these pages. For the SignIn.html page it is:

   ```
   <FORM action="/search_user/" method="Get" TARGET="Main_Frame">
   <p><INPUT TYPE="hidden" NAME="jitUser" VALUE="!jit=0;vlEventID!">
   ```

   You are now signed in as an employee.

4. View the Employee.html Web page that displays from the WebClerk Site Editor.
5. View the StatusSales.html Web page that displays from the WebClerk Site Editor.

Look up Current Activity

1. Click on the Check Your Sales Status link. The StatusSales.html page will display open activities assigned to or initiated by the employee (see Figure 7.2).
2. View the source code in the browser and on the StatusSales.html page via the WebClerk Site Editor.

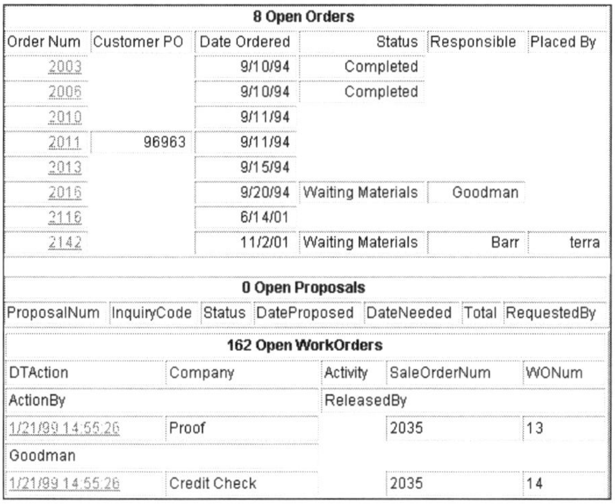

8 Open Orders					
Order Num	Customer PO	Date Ordered	Status	Responsible	Placed By
2003		9/10/94	Completed		
2006		9/10/94	Completed		
2010		9/11/94			
2011	96963	9/11/94			
2013		9/15/94			
2016		9/20/94	Waiting Materials	Goodman	
2116		6/14/01			
2142		11/2/01	Waiting Materials	Barr	terra

0 Open Proposals						
ProposalNum	InquiryCode	Status	DateProposed	DateNeeded	Total	RequestedBy

162 Open WorkOrders				
DTAction	Company	Activity	SaleOrderNum	WONum
ActionBy		ReleasedBy		
1/21/99 14:55:26	Proof		2035	13
Goodman				
1/21/99 14:55:26	Credit Check		2035	14

Figure 7.2 StatusSales.html Web page.

Check Open Orders, Work Orders, and Proposals for Which You Are Responsible

1. Click on any of the active links to view an active Order, Proposal, or Work Order.

Review a List of Customers and Leads That Have Active Follow-Up Requirements

1. In the browser, in the left navigation frame that displays the Web page Index_NavBar.html, click on the Account link. This will return you to the Employee.html page in the right frame. You may also sign in again.
2. With the Employee.html page displayed, you can enter your further search criteria. The defaults on the demo data page offer a search for open items.
3. Click on the Search by Company or Events button.
4. A list of customers, leads, call reports, and service records will be displayed.
5. Click on any record to display its available information.

Find a Specific Customer

1. Click on the Account URL on the Index_NavBar.html page to display the Employee.html page.
2. Enter the company name James. Click on the Search by Company or Events button. Because James Integrated Technologies is assigned to this employee, that database record will display the allowed template.

Place an Order for a Customer via the Web

1. View this feature while the [Customers] record is displayed from Task 5. The CustomerMod.html page is displayed.
2. View CustomerMod.html template from the WebClerk Site Editor or by navigating on the hard drive to the jitWeb folder that is stored under the same folder as the WebClerk application.
3. Note the variable !jit=0;vInAsCustomer! on the CustomerMod.html template. When this template is presented to the browser at the request of someone signed in as a salesperson or sales rep, it is converted to a link:

   ```
   <A HREF="/search_user&userName=terra&Password=jit&*jitUser=376283684*">
   Sign-in As Customer</A>
   ```

4. Click on this URL to convert the person signed in from the salesperson to customer. In the [EventLogs], a record is made that the order was placed by the salesperson in the name of the customer.
5. View the finished order in WebClerk via the Production window.

Conduct a Sales Presentation to a Customer Using the Web

A salesperson can make a limited number of physical sales calls per day but can expand the quantity of quality sales calls via the Web. The Web is not a substitute for personal contact or the personal relationships on which much of business is based. But the Web can extend the capabilities of salespeople to be in touch with more of their customers, more often, and with a persistent presence.

This exercise will walk you, as a customer, through a sales presentation. The written steps are the same as those you would make in a phone call.

1. Before you call the customer, go to the WebClerk application.
2. Close the WebClerk Flow and TechNotes windows if they are open (Click on the X or OK in the upper-left navigation pallet).

3. If you are not at the Sales splash screen go to the Department (Dept) menu and choose Sales.
4. Go to the Customer menu and pull down to Find Customer.
5. Enter James and hit the Tab key. A list of customers whose company begins with James will display.
6. Double click on James Integrated Technologies to open the [Customers] record. In the right center of the screen there is an R with a check box. This notes that there is at least one [RemoteUsers] record for this customer.
7. Click on the check box to display the [RemoteUsers] record. In this demo you will see that there is a record for this customer with the username Terra and password jit. This is the account that will be used in demo.

NOTE

You can create a [RemoteUsers] record by holding down the Alt or Option key and then clicking on the check box. It is permissible to have multiple [RemoteUsers] records for each customer. Each [RemoteUsers] record may have its own authority level and must have a distinct username.

Having internal access to the [Customers] record prior to the sales call lets you see the account balance, order status, proposals, questions and answers (Q&A), customer profile, and other details. With WebSalesForce, a remote salesperson may review these details prior to physical sales or virtual calls. The following is an example script for a Web sales call::

Greetings. Is this a good time to show you our new product line? Do you currently have Web access? We can do this all from your computer.

Please start by launching your Web browser.

In the Address field, I'd like you to enter http://....

While using your machine to host this exercise, enter http://127.0.0.1 and click on Go.

First let me show you how you can see the status of your open orders, open proposals, and recent shipments. On the left-hand side of your browser window, click on the SIGN-IN URL.

The right window will change to display the sign-in page.

NOTE

In this demo, the username (Terra) and password (jit) are already listed as defaults. These default values assure there is data available to be displayed. Under normal circumstances you would have the customer enter a real username and password.

Click on the Submit button.

A page will display showing the account balance. Review this page as desired with the customer. This page is intended to keep customers informed and aid in receivable collection.

On the left frame click on the Status URL.

The OrdStatus.html page will be displayed in the right frame. It shows all the open orders, recent shipments, and open proposals.

Click on Order 2022 to review the specific details of an order.

The OrderOne.html page will be displayed in the right frame. It shows the approved details of an order, the published WorkOrders associated with the order, and an entry form for submitting a service request in support of the order.

The general order information is displayed at the top.

Line item details show current back-order status and expected delivery dates.

There are work orders that show details about tasks that will support completing the order.

These work orders are for a catering event.

At the bottom of the order is a form that you can use to submit service requests about the order. Instead of sending me an email that might not get answered quickly when I am traveling, this service request shows up in our company's order processing system. So even if I am on vacation, your request is handled and the request documented in our corporate memory.

You cannot change your posted order, but service records document the date and time of your requests. If you send a change order, we can act on it. You can see the status of open service requests by pulling up your sales order on the Web.

Your request to change the color scheme has been completed. You can also see this in the work order for the person responsible for managing that task.

[Service] records are created in CommerceExperts' relational database. These records document a service action and track its completion. See Figure A.17 in Appendix A (on the CD) for a graphic representation of service handling. [Service] records may be initiated by the customer, anyone in the company, and outside sales reps. They immediately communicate the request through the company via the My Sales and Service window. They log the actions taken to complete the request.

We have a new line of products I would like to show you. On the left frame, please click on Specials.

The [Items] table is queried for records with a value of Special in the [Items]Profile4 field. The URL is:

```
<A HREF="/item_List?itempro4=Special&*jitUser=!jit=0;vlEventID!*"
TARGET="Main_Frame">SPECIALS</A>
```

Changing the [Items] records can change the list displayed. You can have many categories like this defined by profiles or key words. The use of URLs can keep a sales force tuned to what products are new, changed, or otherwise need to be emphasized. A template page for salespeople can be created that changes as the data in the database changes.

Click on Item Num 111 to display the item.

Discuss with the customer the product image, specification, products that are related to it, and how to access TechNotes. Have him or her click on Demo Movie URL to show an illustration. Repeat this procedure for other products.

Have the customer enter a quantity and submit items to be purchased and click on Check out to complete the order.

Have the customer click on Order Status in the left navigation frame to display the completed order.

Summary

The number and depth of your sales calls can be increased. The Web integrates your traveling sales and work forces.

Case Study 2: Configurable Products

Computers, cars, boats, and many other products have many configurations available. Managing sales of configurable products on the Web is complex. Ordering pizza is used as an example of how to manage complex configurations on the Web. The typical one-page, pizza-ordering sheet—with its choices for different crusts, toppings, and sizes—equates to approximately 30,000 distinct possibilities.

Specification

Objective: Manage configurable products and special offers tied to specific offerings.

Point of Interest:

- Managing choices is applicable to industries from computers to pizza.
- People easily think in terms of a product matrix. Buy a computer, and you choose RAM and drive storage options. Buy a pizza, and you choose the crust, size, multiple toppings, and even what free drink comes with special offers.

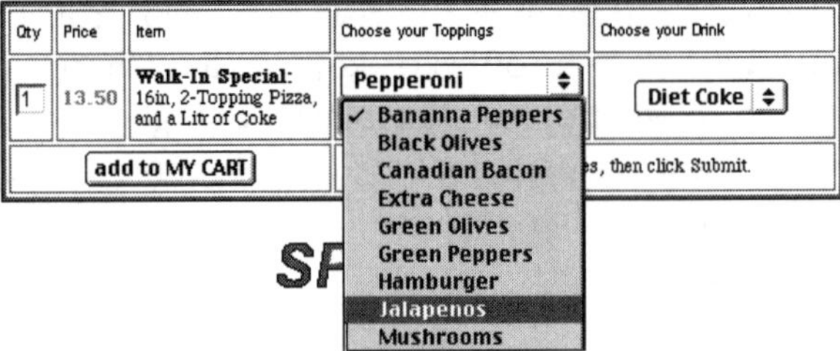

Figure 7.3 Pizza order pop-up list.

- The item illustrated in the pop-up list for a typical pizza order (see Figure 7.3) requires 289 distinct items (2 choices of 17 toppings). A 3-topping pizza with 3 crust sizes equates to 14,739 choices. The choice of any of 3 free drinks tied to this purchase further complicates the computer's management of the order.

Concerns:

- People do not tolerate looking through a long list of distinct choices.
- Computers do not operate well with a matrix of choices. Distinct product codes are needed to track inventory, bills of materials, reorders, and so on.
- It is possible to list the components separately, that is, a 16-inch pizza, a 16-inch serving of pepperoni, a 16-inch serving of jalapenos, and a Diet Coke. But this makes changing an order complex. Bundling items and reorders are impossible with this approach.

Lessons:

- Developing capabilities to manage matrix choices is applicable in a very wide range of industries. Pizza, computers, images, and many other items have options that would require long lists without a choice list approach.
- Web site pages need to be specifically designed to manage multiple choices and have to be limited to specific product groups. For example, separate pages are required for three- and two-topping pizzas. This limits the ability to display products based on the results of searches.
- No marketing effort was made to build awareness for the site. Marketing is required to encourage even existing customers to use a new order-entry method.

Industries: Applicable to a wide variety of industries.

Security: Because payment is made directly to the pizza delivery person, no special security was required. It is possible to operate the site with credit or check on-line payments.

Hardware: The company that implemented this operated on a single iMac computer. Host computers may be either Mac or PC.

Software:

- WebClerk single user was used to manage the business and the site.
- JIT Pricing Matrix, shown in Figure 7.4, was used to create the item numbers.
- Each component of an item number was defined. The appropriate combinations were selected and expanded into unique stock keeping units (SKUs).
- Special consideration was given to the design of the SKUs and was taken into consideration in the design of the Web pages.
- Item numbers begin with the size of the pizza: P12, P14, and so on.
- Toppings were assigned a two-digit number: 42, 43, and so on.
- Users can select any combination in any order and still have the computer resolve that selection to a single SKU.
- These combinations were expanded out to unique items. P12424242 is the unique item number for a 12-inch cheese with three toppings of sausage. P12424243 is the unique item number for a 12-inch cheese with two toppings of sausage and one of pepperoni.

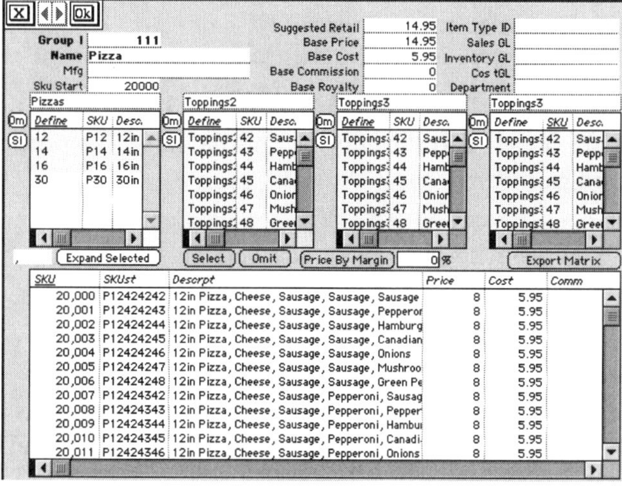

Figure 7.4 JIT Product Matrix application.

Learning Exercise

Place an order on the Web and review the specific HTML pages and the features in WebClerk that support configurable sales.

NOTE

These steps are based on using the WebClerk demo as supplied on the CD accompanying this book. If you have taken actions that will prevent you from having access to the data and features in the demo data, install a new copy and work from the original setup to assure all the components of data, Web pages, and procedures are available.

1. Launch WebClerk in its original installation configuration. See the House Keeping Learning Exercise if you have questions on how to manage the various files.
2. In the WebClerk Flow window, launch the WebClerk Server: click the fourth button under QuickStart.
3. In the WebClerk Flow window open the Site Editor (center-bottom button under Resources); it will open showing the pages in the jitWeb folder.
4. In the Site Editor, scroll down to the ItemSpecial1.html and double-click on it to open the page in the desired HTML editing application. See Learning Exercise: Using the Site Editor for questions on how to use this feature.
5. Review of assembled item number. This Web page displays how to design the Web pages to take advantage of an assembled item number. The item number is initially defined by the first part of the item number, P16. For a pizza with a 16-inch normal crust pizza:

   ```
   <input type="text" name="itemNumP16" value="1">
   ```

   The choice lists on the page assemble the full item number with item extenders. View jitExtend1 and the choices populated with a portion of the remaining item number:

   ```
   <select name="jitExtend1">
   <option value="51">Banana Peppers
   <option value="49">Black Olives
   <option value="45">Canadian Bacon
   <option value="54" selected>Extra Cheese
   <option value="50">Green Olives
   ```

   There are up to 10 item extenders, which are named jitExtend plus a number from 1 to 10 (example: jitExtend1, jitExtend2, through jitExtend10).

The values for the extenders used are sorted prior to combining them into a unique item number or SKU. If a user selected Banana Peppers from the first list (51) and Black Olives (49) from the second, the final unique SKU would still be P164951. This sorting prevents having a different item number for the same exact combination. There cannot be an item number P165149.

6. Review of product bundling. This page also demonstrates the capability for bundling one product with another.

   In the pizza example, it is possible to buy the lunch special and receive a 16-inch two-topping pizza with a free one-liter Coke product. The Web page ItemSpecial1.html is designed to manage this sale in conjunction with WebClerk database records for [Items] and [ItemXRefs].

   The ItemSpecial1.html page is a semifixed page that defines the choices that are possible. The Coke products are added to a choice list named = _Ad1_:

```
<select name="_ad1_">
<option value="Coke Free with Special#11" selected>Coke
<option value="Diet Coke Free with Special#11">Diet Coke
<option value="Sprite Free with Special#11">Sprite
</select>
```

7. The discount is added as a hidden value:

```
<input type="hidden" name="_ad2_" value="discount01#11">
```

   The value passed has two parts. The # separates the components: To its left is the value for [ItemXRefs]ItemNumXRef, and to its right is the [ItemXRefs] XrefLink value.

   The Coke Free with Special and discount01 are used to find matching [ItemXRefs]ItemNumXRef field values. The 11 defines the price point.

   Both values are needed to match with the database records in WebClerk.

8. View the match between the Web page design and the data in WebClerk.
9. Go to the WebClerk application with a splash screen showing.
10. Go to the Action menu >> Search. The Query Editor will display.
11. In the upper left, choose the ItemXRef table from the pop-up list.
12. Build and execute a query for the records with a [ItemXRefs]XrefLinked value of 11. Review the Query Editor details for questions on how to build and execute queries.

    The [ItemXRefs] records that match the Web page will be displayed as shown in Figure 7.5.

ItemXRefs: 8

Item Number	X-Ref Item	Description	SourceID	Lead	Price	Qty	rf	Site	Comment
discount for the W	discount01	-$1.50		0	0	1	11		
SDCoke	Coke Free w	Coke Free with Speci		0	0	1	11		6/12/00: 23:32; C
discount for the Lu	discount02	-$1.10		0	0	1	11		7/8/00: 16:46; Cli
discount on Two 2	discount03	-$1.01		0	0	1	11		
discount 16" 3-To	discount04	-$4.45		0	0	1	11		7/8/00: 16:49; Cli
discount on Two 1	discount05	-$7.01		0	0	1	11		7/8/00: 16:49; Cli
SDSprite	Sprite Free	Sprite Free with Spec		0	0	0	11		
SDDietCoke	Diet Coke Fr	Diet Coke Free with S		0	0	0	11		

Figure 7.5 [ItemXRefs] table output layout of linked items.

13. Double-click on one of these items to display a specific record.
14. Examine how the values on the Web page are lined up with database records.

    These [ItemXRefs] records are further linked to [Items] records by the [ItemXRefs]ItemNum field value. You can click on the Show Related button to display the related [Items] record (Figure 7.6).

    When an order is completed, the inventory and activities of the actual [Items] record is changed. There are [Items] records for both the drinks and discounts. This allows you to track sales and discounts given.

    Up to four bundled items can be attached to any item being ordered. The identifiers are _Ad1_, _Ad2_, _Ad3_ and _Ad4_. In the preceding example the _ad1_ value adds a drink at a price of $0.00. The _ad2_ value adds an item that accounts for the discount of $1.50. The final order has three line items:

    - The pizza being ordered
    - The drink being ordered
    - The discount being applied
15. Close out of these WebClerk windows and return to the Site Editor. Note that you can jump to the Site Editor window by clicking on it in the Process Window (if it is open).

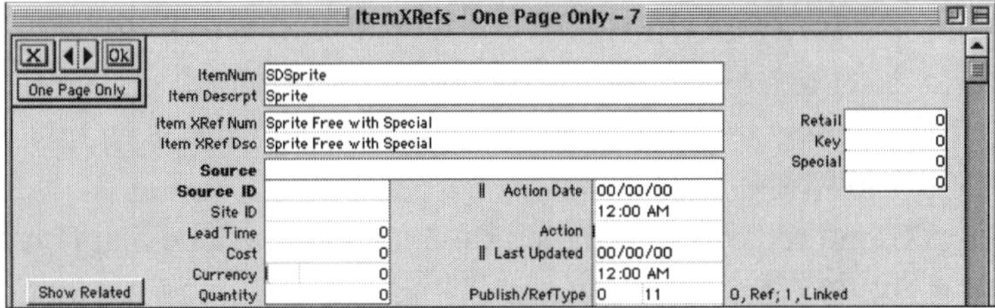

Figure 7.6 [ItemXRefs] table input layout of linked items.

16. Find the Order.html page in the Site Editor.
17. Double-click on it to open it in your preferred HTML editor.
18. Find and view the values for vLineAddShow, vLineAdds and vLineProfiles.

    It is critical that these variables be used on pages that can edit quantity or items ordered. They must be passed between the client and server to keep the bundled items attached to the main item being purchased.

    You do not want the buyer to get the free drink after deleting the pizza purchase. The variables are listed in Table 7.1. The following is a clip of the HTML source code that keeps track of these values:

```
!jit=begin;4;1!
<TR> <TD align=left>
<INPUT TYPE="text" NAME="itemnum!jit=0;p_ItemNum!" VALUE="!jit=0;p_Qty-
Ord!" SIZE=5 length=10></TD>
<TD align=left>!jit=4;7!<BR>!jit=0;vLineAddsShow!</TD>
<TD align=right> !jit=0;p_UnitPrice! </TD>
<TD align=right>!jit=0;p_ExtPrice! <INPUT TYPE="hidden" NAME="thePro-
files" VALUE="!jit=0;vLineProfiles!">
<INPUT TYPE="hidden" NAME="theAdds" VALUE="!jit=0;vLineAdds!"></TD><TD
align=right> </TD></TR>
!jit=end;!
```

19. Go to your browser.
20. Click on the Pizza Demo.
21. Add a special-order pizza with the toppings of your choice.
22. Process the order via your WebClerk server.
23. View the completed order on your browser (Figure 7.7).

Table 7.1 Variables for Managing Bundled Products

VARIABLE	NAME	
vLineAddsShow		Displays comments for the shopper to see.
vLineProfiles	theProfiles	Passes any line profile information back and forth between the server and Web client. Not used with this current order.
VLineAdds	theAdds	Passes bundled item information between the server and Web client. This is used to pass both the discount details and free drink information.

PizzaClerk		James Integrated Technologies 350 East County Road D
Order Num:	228	
Date:	12/1/01	St Paul, MN 55117

Qty	ItemNum	Description	Unit Price	Extended
1	P164358	16in Pizza, Cheese, Pepperoni, Jalepeno	15.00	15.00
1	SDSprite	Sprite Free with Special	0.00	0.00
1	discount for the Walk-In Special	-$1.50	-1.50	-1.50
		Comment		
			Amount	13.50
			Tax	0.81
			Total	14.31

Figure 7.7 Web page OrderCmplt.html displays completed order.

24. Go the WebClerk application and view how the order is displayed on the pizza company's computer. See the Production Editor section for questions.

Summary

Supporting configurable products has great benefits for customers. Long lists that are difficult for users can be consolidated into convenient choices.

Case Study 3: Online Publishing

Dow Jones has been Desktop Hosting reprint sales of *The Wall Street Journal* for several years. It ran its first national ad campaign for its site on May 17, 1999. The company knows the value of publishing in support of its business relationships.

Desktop Hosting can make every business a publisher, even if the only things published are the customer's account balances, order status, and product catalogs. Enriching the customer relationship directly aids your efforts to increase your profitable sales. This ability to support powerful publishing corporations while making the same concepts and tools affordable to every size of business underscores the power of Desktop Hosting. Most businesses can dynamically publish details in support of their trading relationships, shifting unattended communications from message- to published-based.

Publishers obviously know the benefits of publishing. Historically, they have expended considerable resources for printing presses, television stations, and other devices to support their efforts. They are now using the Web to expand the reach of their publications in a symbiotic relationship with public relations companies and with the companies that news affects.

News published has more value than a one-time read. On first print, the data, concepts, product reviews, recommendations, and many other aspects of copyrighted materials are seen only by a limited percentage of the interested population. Dow Jones ran a national ad on this specific topic:

> ***Good News***
>
> *The Wall Street Journal just ran a terrific story about your company in today's paper.*
>
> *Bad News*
>
> *I need to get this article out to my customers, employees, and shareholders today.*
>
> *Great News*
>
> *It's easy! Now you can email or hot-link that story from The Wall Street Journal or Barron's to your company Web page. Now everyone gets to read all about you. Call right now.*

Automating the supply chain of publishers, public relations companies, and news-consuming companies to distribute copyrighted materials to interested viewers is what this case study is about.

Specification

Objective: Profitably sell copyrighted materials in both physical and cyber-space.

Points of Interest: There are two points illustrated by this case study:

- Everyone can be a publisher with the Web. This is an example of how to manage the resale of copyrighted materials and intellectual property.
- Different Web sites can interact to automatically transfer and trade items that are not in the other's systems.

Concerns: Preexecution concerns regarding security and how to handle massive burst hits when many people wanted to see the same story at the same time.

Security: Security issues were managed by implementing the servers with only specific functions enabled. Harmful commands, viruses, worms, and other similar things are meaningless outside the allowed feature set of taking and managing orders.

Traffic: Massive hits were managed by configuring multiple, inexpensive computers to run in parallel as clients to the internal network. A load-distribution device was set as the targeted IP address. Loads were distributed. Additional load was managed by adding more inexpensive computers.

Company:

- Dow Jones, www.djreprints.com, shown in Figure 7.8.
- Reprint Services, http://reprintone.newsclerk.com, also shown in Figure 7.8.

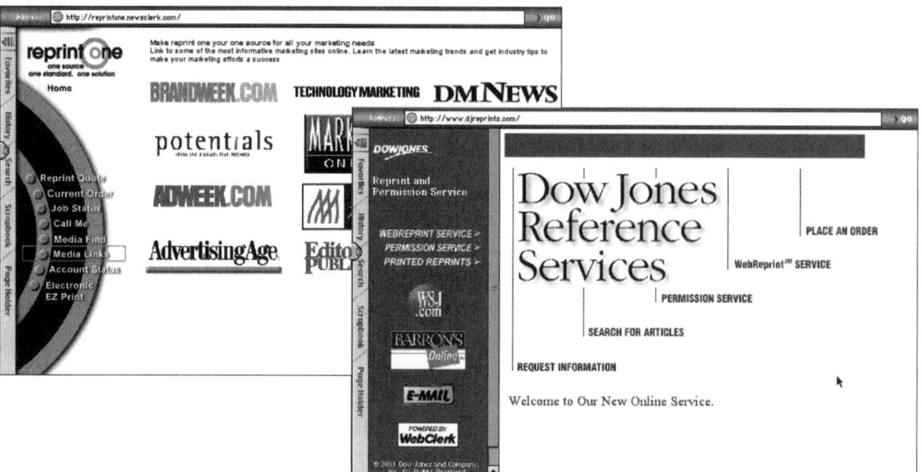

Figure 7.8 NewsClerk and DJReprints Web sites.

NOTE

Disclaimer: There are ongoing revenue relationships between my companies and Dow Jones and Reprint Services. They are referenced here because that is where current experience lies.

Industry: Publishing.

Customers: Public relations and other companies that receive positive press and want to redistribute that copyrighted material to their customers, vendors, shareholders, and others.

Pricing: Pricing for use of copyrighted materials varies by how the product is to be used (newsletters, books, educational materials, paper reprints, electronic format; the length of time the document will be available; quantity ordered; and other factors). Pricing has to adjust to user's choices.

User Comment:

My company is currently using the application both internally and externally.

Internally: Our research department enters "reprint-able" articles into the database as sales prospects, which are followed up on by sales reps.

Externally: The system brings our publishing clients and content repurposing buyers together in a virtual marketplace wherein the buyers are able to instantly purchase content from our online publishers if they have followed the set forth specifications.

In both cases publishers are able to secure additional revenue by making their content accessible to a larger audience.

This ability to sell on the Web for the publishers we support is expanding our ability to recruit new publishers and expand our sales efforts.

Corey Johnson—Reprint Services

General Needs: Manage internal sales and production efforts. Provide Web interface for customers to place orders and check the status of existing orders.

Special Needs: Large numbers of published products that need to be published in multiple ways and in multiple formats, both paper and electronic (in PDF or Web page formats).

Security: Secure transactions are required for credit card processing. WebClerk blocks all actions that are not explicitly permitted, thus protecting the internal network from hackers.

Hardware: The intranet is a standard 10/100 10BaseT network with typical computers. It is a multiplatform environment with both Windows and Macintosh operating systems.

Software:

- Intranet is provided by a CommerceExpert client/server configuration.
- Extranet WebClerk servers are clients to the intranet CommerceExpert server. Additional batteries of the single-user application, HitClerk, individually execute Web serving tasks and periodically coordinate with the commerce application. WebSalesForce is a separate feature that supports field sales force automation.

Special Configurations:

- HitClerk was created to manage massive traffic with standardized, inexpensive computers. Incoming hits are spread across multiple machines. These machines trap the key commercial aspects of the transaction and post the news story to the viewer. Transactional information is then accumulated and passed to the order processing system to consolidate hits, billing, and other commercial details.

- Features were added so that the same publication can be delivered in multiple output formats. A PDF, Quark, HTML, or other document format can be generated automatically based on the intended purpose. This still requires a human review to assure page esthetics.
- A special item documentation mechanism was created so that order entry systems could be separate from the source of the copyrighted materials. Not all published material is worth buying. Some has very limited or special repurposing value. A means for marking all documents without needing to have those documents added as product in an order entry system was required.
- A similar type of specification can be applied to transactions between trading partners where products change quickly. The specification can be applied as either XML or as commented entries in HTML.

NewsClerk Auto-Publishing Specification

Implementation requires a standard interface between data on Web sites and the commerce engine that can manage both physical and Web-based sales.

Interface Specification: Tables 7.2 through 7.4 show listings of some of the specification components and the functions they provide.

Summary: All businesses are publishers. Often what they publish is just catalogs, customer statements, and transactional documents. The Web is a powerful publishing tool that all businesses can use more fully.

Table 7.2 NewsClerk Main Command

COMMAND	FUNCTION	EXAMPLE
/item_create_nc	Command to order article	<A href="/item_create_nc&nc_itemNum=alphNum35&nc_PageOne=&nc_Publisher=BuySellExchange&nc_Title=Carrier-to-Carrier Exchange of Global Telecommunications Capacity&nc_Section=BuySell&nc_URL=http://206.196.63.98/article.html&nc_copyright=unrestricted" target="_blank">Order this page</a>

Table 7.3 NewsClerk Required Parameters

PARAMETERS	FUNCTION
nc_itemNum	Publisher's SKU for the article
Nc_Publisher	Publisher's Unique Identifier
nc_URL_Control	Path to the publishing orders for this document

Table 7.4 Additional Parameters or Comment Markers

PARAMETERS	FUNCTION
nc_PageOne	Page to display the order through.
nc_Publisher	Unique Identifier for each publisher.
nc_Publication	Unique Identifier for each publication.
nc_Section	Identifier for each publication section.
nc_ByLine	Byline.
nc_Title	Title as published.
nc_Market	Market published in.
nc_Date	Date or date and time of publication.
nc_Web_Template	Web template to be used in Web reprints; else, typical layout for this publication and section; else typical layout for the publication; else typical for this publisher, else standard print form.
nc_Print_Template	Print template to be used in paper reprints; else, typical layout for this publication and section; else typical layout for the publication; else typical for this publisher, else standard print form.
nc_Use	Declaration of the how this will be used and for what period; Reprint, pdf, library, local host. Format is `nc_Use=library,3`. This equals library for 3 months.
nc_PriceTable	Declaration of the pricing table to be used in reprinting this item; else, table defined for this publication; else, table defined for the publisher; else, default table; else it becomes $.50 each.
nc_QandA	At order entry creates the typical questions and answers required for reprinting this type of document; else, table for the type of reprint being ordered.
nc_URLOrigin	URL to the original article or object.
nc_URLOnLine	URL to the online article or object.

(continues)

Table 7.4 Additional Parameters or Comment Markers (Continued)

PARAMETERS	FUNCTION
`nc_URLDisplay`	URL to a resell display article or object.
`nc_URLHighRes`	URL to the print quality article or object where this is accessed in combination with a username, password, and known access path to the publisher's primary storage.
`nc_copyright`	General copyright requirement; each object, image, text, movie can have additional requirements. Content commented out tags (must end with a `/nc_...`)
`nc_Content`	Commented out contents to be republished.
`nc_Lead`	Commented out beginning of lead paragraph.
`nc_ByLine`	Commented out by line tag.
`nc_Title`	Commented out Title begin tag.
`nc_Special_##`	Commented out Insert.

Learning Exercise

Convert an article from a portal format into a library link and sell access to that link.

NOTE

These steps are based on using the WebClerk demo as supplied on the CD accompanying this book. If you have taken actions that will prevent you from having access to the data and features in the demo data, install a new copy and work from the original setup to assure all the components of data, Web pages and procedures are available.

1. Launch WebClerk in its original installation configuration. See House Keeping Learning Exercise if you have questions on how to manage the various files.
2. In the WebClerk Flow window, launch the WebClerk Server: Click on the fourth button under QuickStart.
3. In the WebClerk Flow window, open the Site Editor (center-bottom button under Resources). The Site Editor window will open, showing the pages in the jitWeb folder.

4. Scroll down the list to RP_Test.html and double-click on that line to open the page in the HTML editing application of your choice (see Learning Exercise: Using the Site Editor for questions on how to use this feature).

5. RP_Test.html will open in your HTML editor. This page has been designed as though it is being published with or without the use of WebClerk. Any Web server could provide this page (you can see how this command works remotely by going to http://test.newsclerk.com/RP_Test.html).

6. View in the page source for the link `item_create_nc`. This command allows a viewer to order reprints in various formats. For this example, only a link to an HTML page clear of advertising will be shown. Possible formats available are opt-in email, PDF file, printed paper, and others.

   ```
   <A href="/item_create_nc&nc_itemNum=0601sv&nc_PageOne=RP_Buy.html&nc_
   Publisher=TMCNet&nc_Title=YVoIP Keeps Telecommuters, Remote Offices
   Seamlessly Connected To Headquarters&nc_Section=Articles&nc_
   URLArticle=http://www.tmcnet.com/tmcnet/articles/0601sv.htm&nc_
   DisplayBegin= TMC1.ZZZ END &nc_DisplayEnd= TMC2.ZZZ BEGIN &nc_
   copyright=unrestricted" target="_blank">Order this page</a>
   ```

   Parameters passed with this command support the creation of a new item in the commercial database if one does not exist. Only copyrighted materials that have a commercial value beyond their initial publication need to be added to the commercial database, and they are added automatically with the first purchase.

   If you are building pages for a portal site, and if you insert the NewsClerk specified tags, the pages will automatically support the resale of the copyrighted materials.

   Use the RP_Test.html page as a template to build other pages to meet your needs.

   In WebClerk's Site Editor open the NC_OrderItem.html page to view the page that will display to show price points and process the order. The names of the price points relate directly to [TallyResults] records in WebClerk. These records may vary to support different price points for different kinds of copyrighted materials from different publishers.

   ```
   <INPUT TYPE="HIDDEN" NAME="p_LnProfile1" VALUE="Newsclerk">
   Library:<SELECT NAME="p_LnProfile2">
   <OPTION VALUE="1monthlib">1-Month</OPTION>
   <OPTION VALUE="3monthlib">3-Month</OPTION>
   <OPTION VALUE="6monthlib">6-Month</OPTION>
   <OPTION VALUE="1yearlib">1-Year</OPTION>
   <OPTION VALUE="unlmtdlib">Unlimited</OPTION>
   </SELECT>
   ```

In WebClerk, search [TallyResults]Purpose equal to NewsClerk to see where the period price points have been established. The [TallyResults]Name fields have been specified on the NC_OrderItem.html page.

7. Launch your browser.
8. Go to http://127.0.0.1/RP_Test.html. The page will display in your browser.
9. Click on the Order this Page URL. A new page will open, showing an order entry form and key aspects of the copyrighted materials to be purchased.
10. Select a period for the appropriate article and complete the order entry process.
11. The final order will display, giving you a link that you can distribute to those you want to read the article for the period of time that you have purchased access.
12. Switch to the WebClerk application.
13. Search the [Items] table for the item that was created specifically to support the sale of this copyrighted material.

Summary

Merging a physical sales force with Web selling and servicing expands your ability to increase profitable sales. At both Dow Jones and Reprint Services, the physical sales force is integrated directly into the capability to sell on the Web.

This example supports publishers. The following case studies show how every company can benefit by publishing details of its relationships to its trading partners. For more information on using these features access www.newsclerk.com/moreInfo.html.

Case Study 4: Tailor Web Sales to Customer Needs

Selling in ways that customers know you are adding value to their relationship with you.

Specification

Objective: Improve the ability of customers to buy in a way they understand.

Company: The live SEGA site is not listed for you to access during this exercise because of restricted access requirements, but this study exemplifies a method to use Desktop Hosting to satisfy customers' needs 24 hours a day, 7 days a week. SEGA uses this approach in two profit centers, arcade and gaming machine spare parts sales. It is not intended for use by the actual game players, but by companies that service and repair the game units.

User Comment:

"In the first six months of using WebClerk, 50-percent of new orders were placed without the assistance of a Sega customer service representative to assist with order entry,

We project that by the end of the first year, 100-percent of our orders will be placed without order entry assistance. We've already exceeded our ROI with significantly reduced errors, lower costs, and increased customer satisfaction."

Darl Davidson, Sega Corporation

Points of Interest:

- Access to the site is controlled to meet the needs of the relationships.
- Products are presented graphically in exploded assembly drawings so that customers can order by clicking on the desired item.
- Graphical interface reduces order entry errors.
- The graphical presentation can provide direct links to safety instructions, installation movies, and other resources to drive down customer errors or product liabilities.

Concerns:

- Access needs to be limited to only authorized dealers.
- The site must remain unknown to kids who might flood the site with unwanted activity.
- Managers need access to view customer data from remote sites.
- Ways are needed to expand the system to multiple languages.

Lessons:

- Site access can be limited to the needs of the company selling goods and services.
- Graphical ordering drives down the cost of order entry.
- Customers appreciate ordering in a way they understand. SEGA's parts dealers are not generally sophisticated computer operators. Some initial discounts were offered to encourage learning to use the Web. After nearly a year of use, dealers appreciate both the ease and accuracy of ordering.
- Graphical ordering dramatically reduces the number of ordering errors. Web-placed order errors are approaching zero.

Hardware: The intranet is a standard 10/100 10BaseT network with typical computers. It is a multiplatform environment with both Windows and Macintosh operating systems.

Software:

- Intranet is provided by a CommerceExpert client/server configuration.
- Extranet WebClerk servers are clients to the intranet CommerceExpert server. Additional batteries of the single-user application, HitClerk, individually execute Web serving tasks and periodically coordinate with the commerce application. WebSalesForce is a separate feature that supports field sales force automation.

Learning Exercises

Controlling Access

Controlling access is a critical requirement for many business-to-business companies.

- An anonymous Web user has a security level of 1.
- WebClerk can publish resources that have a security (Publish) level of greater than zero.
- To access a resource, a Web visitor must have a [RemoteUsers]SecurityLevel equal to or greater than the [Table]Publish value of the resource.
- SEGA wants limited access to its site and resources. Access is limited by putting the sign-in form (normally on the SignIn.html page) on the Index.html page (the default page for a site).

```
<FORM action="/search_user/" method="Get" TARGET="Main_Frame">
<p><INPUT TYPE="hidden" NAME="jitUser" VALUE="!jit=0;vlEventID!">
<INPUT TYPE="text" NAME="userName" VALUE=" " size="25">
<INPUT TYPE="password" NAME="password" VALUE=" " size="25">
<input type="submit" name="name" value="Sign In"></FORM>
```

  - When this page is submitted with an authorized username and password, a [RemoteUsers] record sets the SecurityLevel of access for further access and returns the Customer.html page. This page displays the customer's account balance and gives further access to permitted resources.
  - The Error.html page is returned with an incorrect username or password combination.
  - When people sign in, the authorization levels in their [RemoteUsers]SecurityLevel records are noted. Access to features and pages is allowed based on that authority level. Users can only see resources for which their access level is equal to or greater than the Publish value of the resource.

- HTML pages further limit access if a jitSecurity level is declared in their templates. The following are two examples of this declaration that require the [RemoteUsers]SecurityLevel to be 4 or more:

```
<META name=jitPageSecurity content=!jitSecure=4!>
<!-!jitSecure=4!"->
```

- An error message is returned if a page exists and is called but is not within the authority of the [RemoteUsers]SecurityLevel.

Graphical Order Entry

Graphically presenting ordering information in ways understood by buyers is powerful. Mechanics understand exploded parts diagrams as shown in Figure 7.9. Ordering spare parts by clicking on the exploded parts diagram is clearly understood. The addition of a photo of each part further assures the correct item is being ordered. Unlike many Web shopping carts, the diagram needs to stay on the screen until the mechanic is finished ordering parts for the device. Frames manage the order entry details separate from the diagram being ordered from.

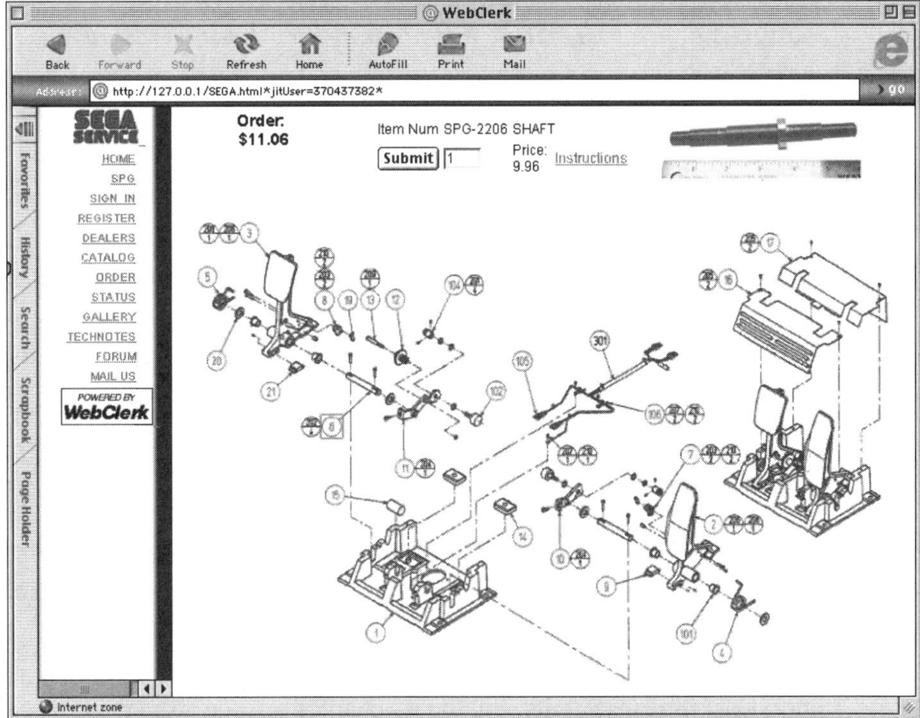

Figure 7.9 Exploded assembly diagram as active Web page.

Designing graphical order entry is done by several mechanisms:

Java applets. These are special programs that enable browsers to perform tasks not programmed into their basic functions.

Frames. This is the method displayed in the preceding code (a Java applet could look identical). This frame set is displayed in the demo included with the book by calling http://127.0.0.1/sega.html. This page creates four frames in two steps. The first step creates the Navigation and Main frames:

```
<frameset cols="119,*" border=0 frameborder=0 framespacing=0>
<frame src="/SEGA_NavBar.html?*jitUser=!jit=0;vlEventID!*"
name="Nav_Frame" marginwidth="0" marginheight="0" scrolling="auto"
frameborder="no" noresize>
<frame src="/SEGAMapFrames.html&*jitUser=!jit=0;vlEventID!*"
name="Main_Frame" marginwidth="0" marginheight="0" scrolling="auto"
frameborder="no" noresize>
</frameset>
```

The SEGAMapFrames.html creates the second set of three frames:

```
<frameset rows="80,*" border=1>
<frameset Cols="25%,*" border=1>
<frame name="Ord_Frame" src="/SEGAOrderSM.html*jitUser=!jit=0;
vlEventID!*" marginwidth="0" marginheight="0" scrolling="no"
frameborder="yes">
<frame name="Frame_PDescript"
src="/SEGAExplainOne.html*jitUser=!jit=0;vlEventID!*" marginwidth="10"
marginheight="10" scrolling="No" frameborder="yes" noresize>
</frameset>
<frame name="L_Frame" src="/SEGA_SPG-2200.html*jitUser=!jit=0;
vlEventID!*" marginwidth="10" marginheight="10" scrolling="Auto"
frameborder="no"></frameset
```

The URL uses these frames to process the order:

```
http://127.0.0.1/item_List?itemNum=SPG-2215&jitPageOne=
SEGAItemFrameRec.html&*jitUser=376803853*
```

Each balloon is tied to a specific item. Clicking on that balloon targets the Frame_Pdescript frame with the SEGAItemFrameRec.html page and the data for the part number SPG-2215. In addition the jitUser server-side tag maintains continuity with user actions.

Designing these pages in HTML is managed by taking images and placing links in concert with the image.

Link mapping is accomplished as shown in Figure 7.10, using the Macromedia Dreamweaver Web page editor. This image connects the database [Items]ItemNum with the graphical presentation on the Web.

Mechanics order by clicking on the item they need. With a local maintenance shop Desktop Hosting its site, the mechanics can see if the item is available. They can access the information from a computer connected to the Web or

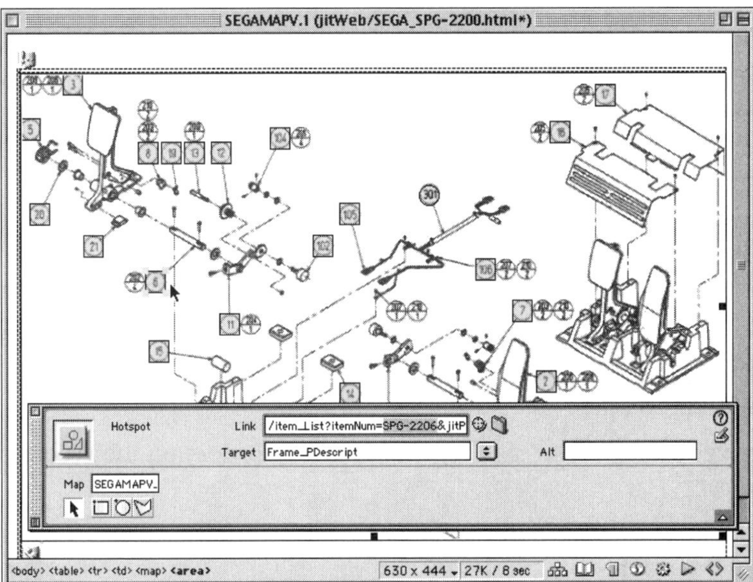

Figure 7.10 Exploded assembly diagram in Dreamweaver.

from a wireless device, such as the Compaq iPAQ, as shown in Figure 7.11. The parts manager can search other local shops for product availability.

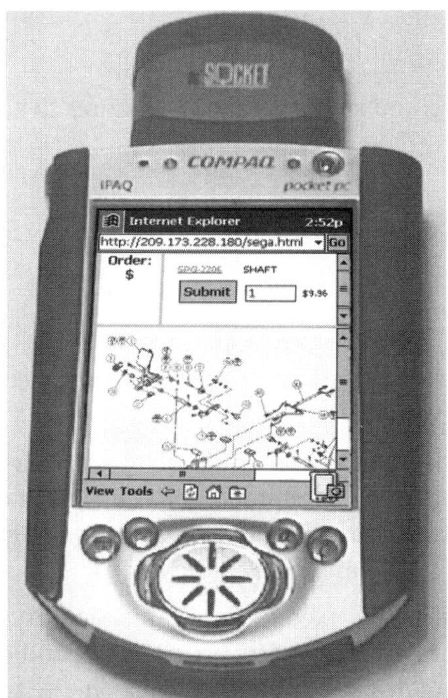

Figure 7.11 iPAQ as a wireless order entry tool.

Summary

Putting the point of communications at the point of action, using the power of browsers to give customers an interface matched to their sense of value, adds to profit.

Case Study 5: Small Retailer and Shipping

Location, Location, Location. Locating inventory (physical and virtual) on your customer's computer is about to become critical for retailers, as in these simple examples:

- The pizza store whose cash register is taking orders on the Web as it rings up sales.
- A kid who shows his parents the exact bike from the on-hand inventory of a local bike store.

Desktop Hosting is empowering all businesses to sell and service their customers on the Web. It will not create new customers and destroy the existing distribution channels as was projected before the dot.com meltdown. It will enhance the primary reasons there are retailers in the first place: location and service.

This case study is about a small candy retailer in California.

Specification

Objective: Create a profitable mechanism for local candy stores to sell via the Web.

Point of Interest:

- Very limited budget.
- Adjustments to high burst loads when featured on Food TV.

Concerns:

- Food TV was running a special on the store's nostalgic candy selection. A burst of interest was expected.
- The site had to be built in two months to include pictures of more than 1000 pieces of candy. Project activities included enabling credit card processing, entering inventories, learning programs, interfacing with United Parcel Service (UPS), and many other specifics.
- It had to be put together on a small, fixed budget. This included the seven-seat client/server CommerceExpert enterprise sales and operations software to manage the sales and inventory, plus on-site training.
- Ongoing support and modifications had to be paid for by profits.

Lessons: Technical

- We knew this was stupid and we did it anyway: Insignificant wording changes were jamming our resources right up to the launch of the Food TV broadcast. They occupied a significant part of the available bandwidth when the wave of customers responded to the broadcast. Result: Most of the images were unavailable during the first response.
- The battery of overload servers was never engaged because the site modifications could not be transferred.
- The bandwidth ordered was DSL 512 kilobytes. The provider stated the change was made. It was still at 128 kilobytes when the wave hit. It was further constricted at the third or fourth bounce point within the provider's network. Not testing was the direct result of consuming resources rewriting pages up to the last minute.
- The broadcasts occurred on a weekend. Access to the load-spreading mechanism and the image farm needed to be up. All changes had to be pushed through a network alrcady loaded with customer interest.
- Spreading the load of burst events (response to broadcast) does work; however, executing it requires resources to be debugged and tested before the onset of the event.
- Once changes were complete, locating heavy graphics at a data farm with very high bandwidth was a very good move. Had we not still been moving them during the first broadcast, it would have been perfect. The Web site has many images, but the capabilities of the graphics server farm did not even come close to being exceeded.
- Interface with carriers can be very dynamic. In this case, information is posted most frequently to UPS World Ship. The tracking numbers are returned so that customers can view their recent shipments by clicking on a URL. Internal customer service can track the packages by finding a customer's record in the database and posting a request to UPS. See TechNote: UPS Inter Activity.

Lessons: Business

- Keep priorities in mind when approaching a major event.
- The plan was for a fixed cost to ship. That was inadequate because chocolate and wax lips orders required overnight shipping. Even then, orders were damaged sitting in vans. The site was changed so that the customer had the option to change carrier or shipping method to match the order. A warning screen is also now used to advise customers of summer shipping requirements.
- A very small percentage of customers cannot be pleased. Interacting remotely with these people can consume all the profits made from all the other satisfied customers.

- Similar to FTD in the flower industry, the long-term intent is to rent this data set and the technology to a large number of candy retailers. Orders can be taken at any retailer. Delivery and service may be managed by the retailer nearest the customer. The ultimate benefit: national selling presence, local support.

Company: California Candy Company, www.californiacandy.com. Figure 7.12 illustrates the appearance of its Web site.

Industry: Candy, retail.

Customers: Consumers, gift buyers, and corporate gift buyers.

Pricing: Pricing is set at different levels for price quantity breaks, wholesale to other retailers, and commercial buyers. Buyers have a remote user record that identifies what price point they are to receive.

General needs: Manage internal sales. Coordinate between inventory in the retail store and mail order. Interface with UPS for shipping. Manage customer relations.

Security: An SSL connection is established during the credit card information transfer.

Figure 7.12 www.CaliforniaCandy.com. Web site for selling candy from a retailer.

Hardware: The intranet is a standard 10/100 10BaseT network with typical computers. It is a multiplatform environment with both Windows and Macintosh operating systems.

Software:

- Intranet is provided by a CommerceExpert client/server configuration.
- Extranet WebClerk servers are clients to the intranet CommerceExpert server. Additional batteries of the single-user application, HitClerk, individually execute Web serving tasks and periodically coordinate with the commerce application. During heavy traffic events, the load is spread to remote, single-user WebClerks. Data is then synchronized among the sites.

Learning Exercises

An example of the features used by California Candy is the shipping function. Its CommerceExpert server connects to its UPS machine to support shipping and customer service of shipping details. The following example defines the mechanics of this.

Order Flow

- Orders and credit cards are taken on the phone or via the Web.
- Inventories are managed within CommerceExpert, goods are accumulated, and orders prepared for shipment.
- When the goods for an order are ready to ship, the credit card number that was captured at order entry time is processed. If the credit card is approved, the order is invoiced. This step is actually done on a batch of orders each day.
- Invoice Details to UPSInvoice details are passed on the UPS computer from CommerceExpert, an exported text document is created with the details, and this script is executed as a [UserReports] record, as follows:
    1. Pull up a list of [Invoices] records.
    2. Go to File menu >> Print Defined Report. A list of reports for the [Invoices] table will display.
    3. Double-click on the report named Export JIT_2_UPS. This report is type EDIX, or an executable action. It creates a text file that can be imported into UPS. View the document created in any spreadsheet or text-editing program. It is stored in the UPS folder in the same directory as the WebClerk application.

NOTE

You may view the script code that is executed by clicking on the Report Setup button in the report selection window.

A TechNote at www.WebClerk.com shows how to set up UPS software to accept this file. It is not presented here because UPS may change the requirements. Documentation available on the Web can keep pace with changes.

Tracking Details from UPS to CommerceExpert

From the UPS program you can create a file that posts back into CommerceExpert the shipping details.

1. From the splash screen go to the File menu >> Print Defined Report. A list of predefined reports will display.
2. Double-click on the report named !UPS2JIT import. This will execute a script to import a file created by UPS software and bring the tracking numbers into CommerceExpert.

NOTE

You may view the script code that is executed by clicking on the Report Setup button in the Report Selection window.

Customer Support for Shipper Tracking

1. From the Sales splash screen go to the Ord menu and select Search by Order#. A window opens for entering a specific order number.
2. Enter 2022 and click on OK button. The demo order 2022 will open.
3. Go to the File menu >> Print Defined Report. A window will open showing defined reports for the [Orders] table.
4. Double-click on the report named !UPS IE Post if you use Internet Explorer as your browser or !UPS Nav Post if you use Netscape Navigator. CommerceExpert will query any invoices associated with the order and further query any shipping records associated with any of the invoices. This information will be posted into an HTML page that has the correct format for submitting requests to the shipper.

The following is the HTML code built and displayed for submission to UPS. The same type form may be submitted to FedEx, Airborne, USPS, or other shipper that allows Web-based tracking of packages.

```
<HTML>
<HEAD>
<TITLE>UPS Package Tracking</TITLE>
</HEAD>
<BODY BGCOLOR="#FFFFCC" TEXT="#333333" LINK="#0033CC" ALINK="#3399FF"
VLINK="#990000">
<FORM ACTION="http://wwwapps.ups.com/etracking/tracking.cgi"
METHOD="GET"><A NAME="top">top</A>
<INPUT TYPE="HIDDEN" NAME="tracknums_displayed" VALUE="10">
<INPUT TYPE="HIDDEN" NAME="TypeOfInquiryNumber" VALUE="T">
<INPUT TYPE="HIDDEN" NAME="HTMLVersion" VALUE="4.0">
<INPUT TYPE="HIDDEN" NAME="sort_by" VALUE="status">
<TABLE BORDER="0" CELLSPACING="0" CELLPADDING="2" WIDTH="261">
<TR><TD colspan=2><B>Tracking Numbers:</B></TD></TR>
<TR>
<TD>1.</TD><TD><INPUT TYPE="TEXT" NAME="InquiryNumber1" SIZE="24"
MAXLENGTH="24" value="1ZThisIsTheTrackingN"></TD></TR>
<TR><TD>2.</TD><TD><INPUT TYPE="TEXT" NAME="InquiryNumber2" SIZE="24"
MAXLENGTH="24" value=""></TD></TR>
<TR><TD>3.</TD><TD><INPUT TYPE="TEXT" NAME="InquiryNumber3" SIZE="24"
MAXLENGTH="24" value=""></TD></TR>
<TR><TD>4.</TD><TD><INPUT TYPE="TEXT" NAME="InquiryNumber4" SIZE="24"
MAXLENGTH="24" value=""></TD></TR>
<TR><TD>5.</TD><TD><INPUT TYPE="TEXT" NAME="InquiryNumber5" SIZE="24"
MAXLENGTH="24" value=""></TD></TR>
<TR><TD>6.</TD><TD><INPUT TYPE="TEXT" NAME="InquiryNumber6" SIZE="24"
MAXLENGTH="24" value=""></TD></TR>
<TR><TD>7.</TD><TD><INPUT TYPE="TEXT" NAME="InquiryNumber7" SIZE="24"
MAXLENGTH="24" value=""></TD></TR>
<TR><TD>8.</TD><TD><INPUT TYPE="TEXT" NAME="InquiryNumber8" SIZE="24"
MAXLENGTH="24" value=""></TD></TR>
<TR><TD>9.</TD><TD><INPUT TYPE="TEXT" NAME="InquiryNumber9" SIZE="24"
MAXLENGTH="24" value=""></TD></TR>
<TR><TD>10.</TD><TD><INPUT TYPE="TEXT" NAME="InquiryNumber10" SIZE="24"
MAXLENGTH="24" value=""></TD></TR>
<TR>
<TD colspan=2 align="Center">
<INPUT TYPE="submit" NAME="track" VALUE="Submit"></TD>
</TR>
</TABLE>
</FORM>
</HTML>
```

NOTE

Internet Explorer will launch automatically if configured to do so on your system.

Submitting this page will return the current status of the shipment listed to the browser of the customer service person contacted about the shipment. The customer can also directly access this shipping information by signing in to the Web site. Recent shipments are displayed when a customer clicks on the Status URL.

In the demo data set, while running the WebClerk server, do the following exercise.

Customer Views Recent Shipments

1. Launch your browser.
2. Enter the URL http://127.0.0.1
3. In the left frame click on Sign-in URL. The right frame will display the SignIn.html page with the username Terra and password jit.
4. Click on the Submit button. The account for James Integrated Technology will display.
5. In the left frame, click on the Status URL. The right frame will display the OrdStatus.html page with the open orders, recent shipments, and open proposals.
6. Click on a recent shipment. The page will change based on the first three characters of the shipper. It explains the rules for tracking a package.
7. Clicking on the Submit button returns the tracking information for the shipment.

Summary

- Desktop Hosting is applicable to companies regardless of size.
- The Web effectively opens a retail store to 24 hours a day, 7 days a week.
- Desktop Hosting adds a customer's computer to the locations to which the company can provide service and support.
- As shown in Case Study 7, Desktop Hosting simplifies the technology difficulties of small business. High-quality current data is updated to the local retailer for a minor rental fee. This data set becomes a Common-Language between trading partners. This is similar to the data set of available airline seats provided by companies like Sabre.

Case Study 6: Desktop Hosting for Profit Centers

The fundamental objective of for-profit companies is profit. This case study uses hotels to demonstrate how to apply Desktop Hosting concepts and technology to support the varied profit centers in a single business. This permits the profit centers to concentrate on adding value for which customers will pay.

Specification

Objective: Provide specific capabilities so that the many different profit centers that make up a hotel can transact with their varied customers.

Points of Interest:

- A hotel is a single business with many varied profit centers. Each of these profit centers has its own products and services. Each supports customers that may or may not overlap with the customer base of others. Specific details must be correct and coordinated so that events planned at hotels meet the needs of the customers by the deadline of the events. Figure 7.13 illustrates the many separate but interrelated profit/customer service centers in a hotel.
- In many ways a hotel is a miniature economy. This case study looks at integrating these profit centers with a Web-centric approach.

Concerns: The system needs to be secure so that only authorized people can make modifications to the site. Salespeople need to be selling, and the interface to their information should not impede their productivity.

Lessons:

- This effort has been designed, but has yet to be implemented in a hotel system. The lessons listed are those projected based on efforts in other areas. We expect implementations of this to begin in 2002.
- Operating from profit centers simplifies the task of implementing systems.
- Web pages from multiple sites must be combined so that the various tasks of multiple profit centers can display in a customer-centric way.

Company: Not yet implemented. The concepts were presented to and well-received by a group of hotel executives in Hong Kong in November 2001.

Industry: Hotel and hospitality industry.

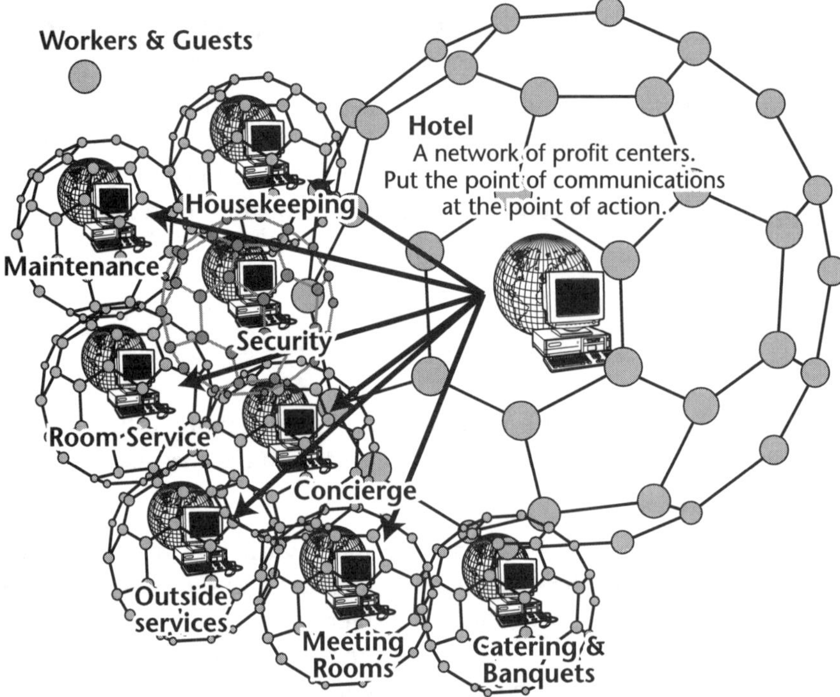

Figure 7.13 Multiple profit centers are connected into a network that provides service and information to hotel guests and workers.

General Needs:

- A hotel has many functions, each of which can have radically different customer bases, tasks to perform, and products and services.
- The wide variety of products and services must be managed within an affordable technology budget. Wireless access to schedules, workloads, and emergency messages is needed because it is very important to coordinate last-minute changes with the activities of the many people involved in servicing events.

Security: Requirements for secure financial transactions are typical. It is important to prevent hackers from changing event activities or key facts. Use it in support of security staff is an area of interest. Wireless networks and wearable PCs make it possible for the security chief at a large facility to wear the Web server. Active personnel can report current status, location, and other factors to this mobile server.

Hardware:

- The intranet is a standard 10/100 10BaseT network with typical computers. Those with standard browsers, palm devices, and cell phones must be able to view the extranet.
- The wearable PC we tested is made by Via. It is an 800-megahertz PC with the Windows operating system and a 40-gigabyte hard drive. It is likely that this technology is going to be valuable for Desktop Hosting solutions in which mobility extends beyond using palm devices to control a desktop machine. See Case Study 7 for more discussion about wireless network implementation.
- Cell phones are especially important for the hotel staffs, servers, and outside services. Messaging via cell phones allows coordination of complex events without massive changes in available hardware.
- See also the networking discussion in Case Study 7.

Software:

- Intranet is provided by a CommerceExpert client/server configuration.
- Extranet servers are clients to the intranet server, using the combined features of CommerceExpert and WebClerk. The jitWeb folder in these implementations must have matching jitWebCE and jitWebCell folders. These additional folders project the same information that is visible to a standard browser, but the pages are tailored to display on the smaller screens of Windows CE palm devices and cell phones.

Scenarios

A hotel is effectively a miniature city. The following scenarios and exercises demonstrate how to use Desktop Hosting to support different profit centers. Beyond the hotel itself, there are other businesses whose services the hotel should publish as a value-added service to their guests.

Economic Community: Concierge

Hotel guests at a convention need to know such things as where to park, the best places to meet a group of people, and what restaurants, entertainment, and radio stations are in the area. Desktop Hosting provides the concierge with answers. WebClerk has a set of features for managing and publishing information about companies. For manufacturing and distribution companies, this provides a means of publishing dealer locator functions. For a concierge, it provides a means of accessing and publishing details tailored to the economic community, such as an interactive telephone book.

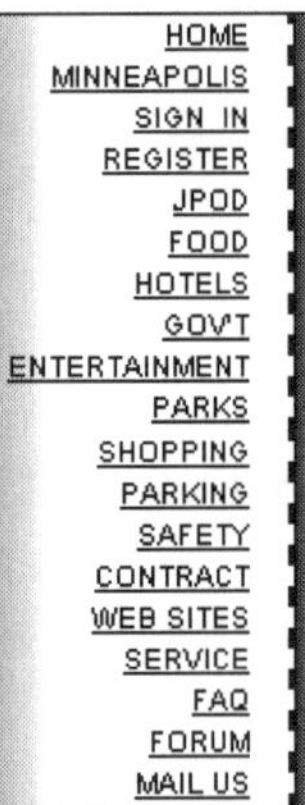

Figure 7.14 A concierge's site may display these navigation links.

The navigation links shown in Figure 7.14 permit company profiles to be searched in the local database; then the company's Web site can be queried to gather the latest updates, and the results presented to the guest. Entertainment, theaters, nightclubs, bars, sports events, restaurants (by type, price range, dress code, and so on) are obvious examples of businesses that would like to have their information accessible. As businesses activate their Desktop Hosting sites, details on their services are published to their economic community.

Coordinating the Distributed Capacity of Parking Lots

Desktop Hosting concepts may be used to effectively communicate the distributed capacity of space as an inventory, specifically that of parking space in a metropolitan area. Parking lots are rarely considered publishers. Nearly every driver has been faced with full-lot signs when in a hurry to get parked for an important meeting or appointment. If parking ramps and lots with available spaces could be displayed in a map, such as shown in Figure 7.15, the driver could log on and prepay for a parking spot before leaving the hotel.

Reserving a parking space near the driver's destination on a 100-degree day benefits both the vehicle owner and the parking business. The parking lot will rent a space not yet filled, and the driver will not have to run eight blocks in a suit to get to a meeting.

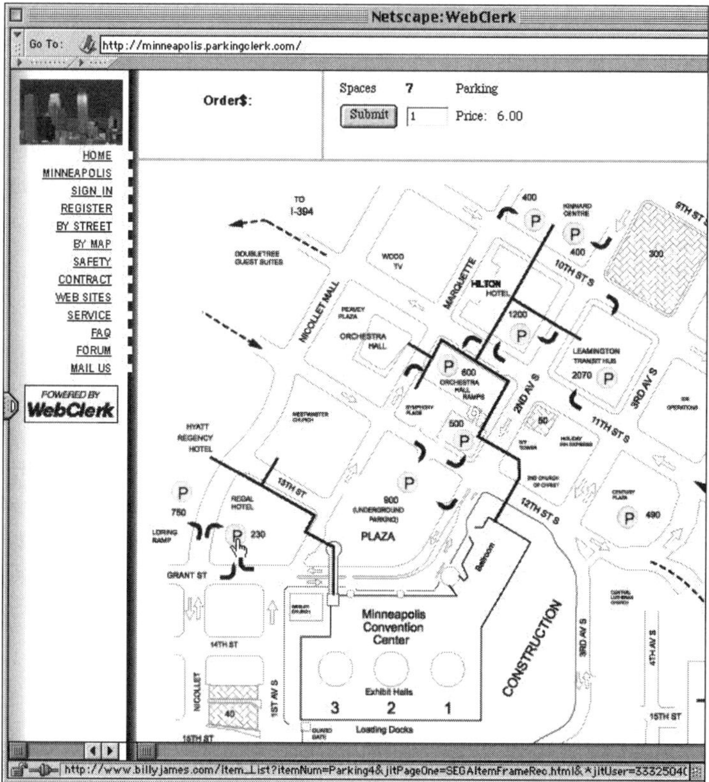

Figure 7.15 A concierge Web site displays interactive updates to available parking in metropolitan parking ramps and lots.

Learning Exercise

1. Open your Web browser with WebClerk serving its default page.
2. Click on the EXAMPLE link. A new window will open listing a number of example sites.
3. Click on the ParkingClerk link; the ParkingClerk demo page will display.
4. Click on any of the yellow circles to display the current number of open parking spaces. On a live site, the open spaces can display over the picture of the parking lot.

NOTE

This site functions by calling the [Items] table on the local machine. Visit www.ParkingClerk.com to download examples that are more dynamic.

Initially, it is expected that individual parking lots will not run their own Web servers. They will use a telephone or modem to report the number of open spaces to a centralized ParkingClerk server.

The ParkingClerk approach can also be applied to van pools, park-and-ride share programs, and other efforts to reduce traffic congestion.

Catering Group Profit Center

The sales order is an electronic record of the business transaction among the profit centers, customers, workers, and vendors. For this exercise, we will use an order that is already in the CommerceExpert/WebClerk database, order 2120. We will capture a customer order to cater a meeting with wine and follow the activities of the hotel's catering staff.

Learning Exercise

1. Start WebClerk. If the WebClerk Flow page displays, click on Launch WebClerk.
2. Close the WebClerk Flow and TechNotes windows by clicking on the X in the Navigation Pallet in the upper left of the screen. The Sales splash screen will still bc displayed.
3. Go to the Ord menu >> Search by Order#. A dialog window will open the search for a specific order. Type in 2120 and click the OK button. The database will search for and display [Orders] record with [Orders]OrderNum equal to 2120 (see Figure 7.16).
4. Hold the Control key (Command key for Mac) down and type R or go to the Actions menu >> Relate Files to make sure records related to this order are displayed in their windows. (This step be automatic. There is a program default that gives users the choice to turn the Auto-Relate mechanism on or off).
5. Click on and drag through the line items (center of screen).
6. Click on the L button on the left of the screen. The current inventory level of these items will list at the bottom of the screen. In the left (navigation) frame, click on the Sign-in URL. There is no inventory of the Firstland Cabernet or the Pierre Sparr Riesling. In Case Study 7, you will process a purchase order to buy these wines.

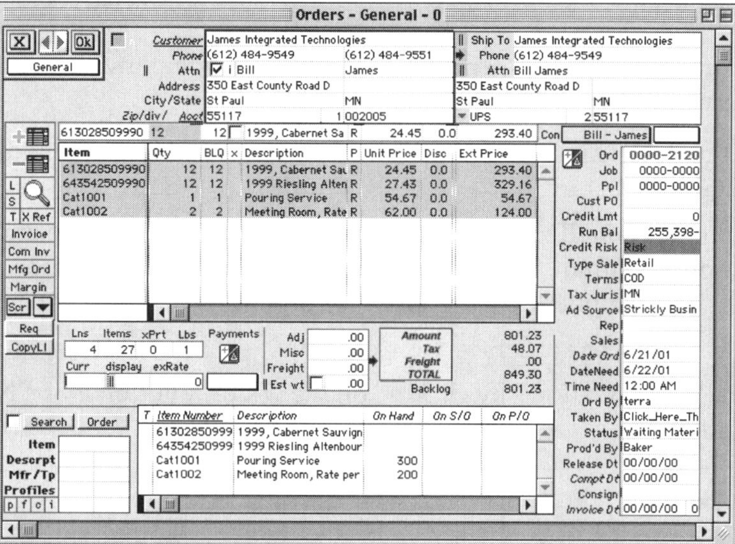

Figure 7.16 Sales Order 2120.

7. Go to the Navigation Pallet (upper-left corner). Click on the General pop-up, drag down to the WO's/Time page, and release the mouse button. The page will change to the WO's/Time page. The current [WorkOrders] records related to this sales order are displayed in the lower right. You may add/subtract [WorkOrders] (Figure 7.17).
8. View the details of the Bar Setup WorkOrder for Goodman by double-clicking on the line item. The WorkOrders Input Layout record will display.
9. You may add comments. You should leave this record published (value of 1 in the Pub field on the right center). As elsewhere in WebClerk, this is the authority level that is allowed to see a record on the Web.
10. Click on the OK button in the Navigation Pallet (upper left) to close the WorkOrder. It will return you to order 2120.
11. Click on the OK button in the Navigation Pallet to close the order.

WO's + − complete cmd/reclose; alt /clear

c	Descriptic	Activity	NameID	Dt Need	Dt Cmpl
p	Colors:Th	Decoration	Barr	6/22/01	00/00/00
p	Projector	AV	Goodman	6/22/01	00/00/00
p	Customer	Music	McConnell	6/22/01	00/00/00
p	Entertainr	Entertainmer	Barr	6/22/01	00/00/00
p	Bar Setup	Bar	Goodman	6/22/01	00/00/00

Figure 7.17 WorkOrders are listed in Order 2120.

Learning Exercise

People can manage the workloads within a company by using the Client/Server configuration of CommerceExpert:

1. Go to the Review menu >> Workload. The Workload layout will display (see Figure 7.18).
2. Click on the NameID pop-up in the top center; drag it down to and release on Goodman. The current open work orders for Goodman will display. You can find the work order for order 2120.
3. Open various work orders to view contents.
4. Close all open windows by clicking on the OK or X button in the Navigation Pallet.

Learning Exercise

To view the open activities for Goodman on the Web, in this exercise we will use a standard browser. It is currently possible to use a handheld wireless device instead of a computer. A cell phone interface for workers to manage their workloads from the Web has been tested and will be released to the market in 2002.

1. Call up your demo site on your computer (make sure WebClerk is serving).
2. Sign-in with username Employee and password Test. The Employee.html page will display with the capability to search for additional information.
3. Click on thc URL Show Sales Activities. Open Orders, Proposals, and WorkOrders assigned to Goodman will display. Employees can manage their workload, report back to the order any work completed, and access the order and customer records.

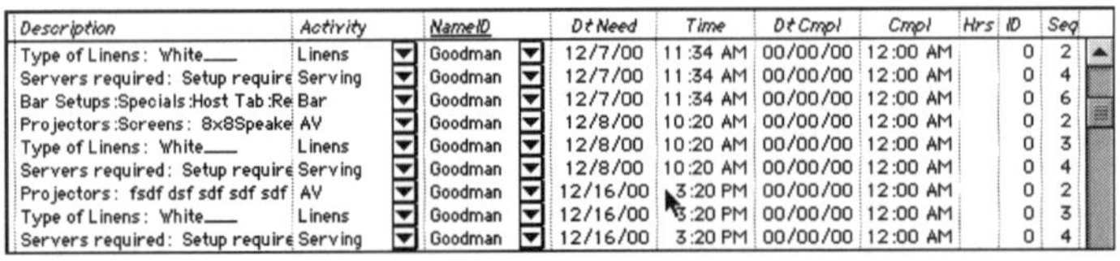

Description	Activity	NameID	DtNeed	Time	DtCmpl	Cmpl	Hrs	ID	Seq
Type of Linens: White___	Linens	Goodman	12/7/00	11:34 AM	00/00/00	12:00 AM		0	2
Servers required: Setup require	Serving	Goodman	12/7/00	11:34 AM	00/00/00	12:00 AM		0	4
Bar Setups:Specials:Host Tab:Re	Bar	Goodman	12/7/00	11:34 AM	00/00/00	12:00 AM		0	6
Projectors:Screens: 8x8Speake	AV	Goodman	12/8/00	10:20 AM	00/00/00	12:00 AM		0	2
Type of Linens: White___	Linens	Goodman	12/8/00	10:20 AM	00/00/00	12:00 AM		0	3
Servers required: Setup require	Serving	Goodman	12/8/00	10:20 AM	00/00/00	12:00 AM		0	4
Projectors: fsdf dsf sdf sdf sdf	AV	Goodman	12/16/00	3:20 PM	00/00/00	12:00 AM		0	2
Type of Linens: White___	Linens	Goodman	12/16/00	3:20 PM	00/00/00	12:00 AM		0	3
Servers required: Setup require	Serving	Goodman	12/16/00	3:20 PM	00/00/00	12:00 AM		0	4

Figure 7.18 The client Workload screen shows a list of activities and their schedule for completion.

Summary

Because profit centers are where profit can be tracked, implement technology and business solutions at the profit-center level, and knit them together by reporting at the general-ledger level. When different profit centers have different customers, relationships, transaction types, goods, and services, give them the tools to make profitable selling their first priority. A one-size-fits-all approach may aid the information technology staff, but it often does not provide enough flexibility to meet the primary responsibility of a for-profit corporation, which needs to add more value than the cost to compete. There are so many details to manage in order to be profitable, putting "the leaves at the end of the branches" permits those who care about the details to use and maintain those details.

The examples and exercises show that:

- Perishable information is valuable when published. Examples include the availability of tickets, parking spaces, menus, and reservations.
- Every business can benefit from becoming a publisher.
- Many hands make light work. Breaking a large business or economic community into its profit centers, engaging the self-interest of those involved, and tailoring technology to increase profitable sales by profit center is both simple and valuable.
- Simple is achievable.
- Added value adds to profit (costs are kept in control).

Case Study 7: Supply Chain Automation

By empowering everyone and focusing on profit centers, Desktop Hosting enables entire supply chains to automate.

Specification

Objective: Automate the supply chain in the fine wine industry: Change it from islands of data and technology into a sales flow with a Common-Language and Common-Tools. Figure 7.19 shows how the data and technology are interrelated.

Company: Wine Operations, Inc. (WineOps), www.WineOperations.com or www.WineOps.com.

Industry: Supply chain automation for the beverage industry.

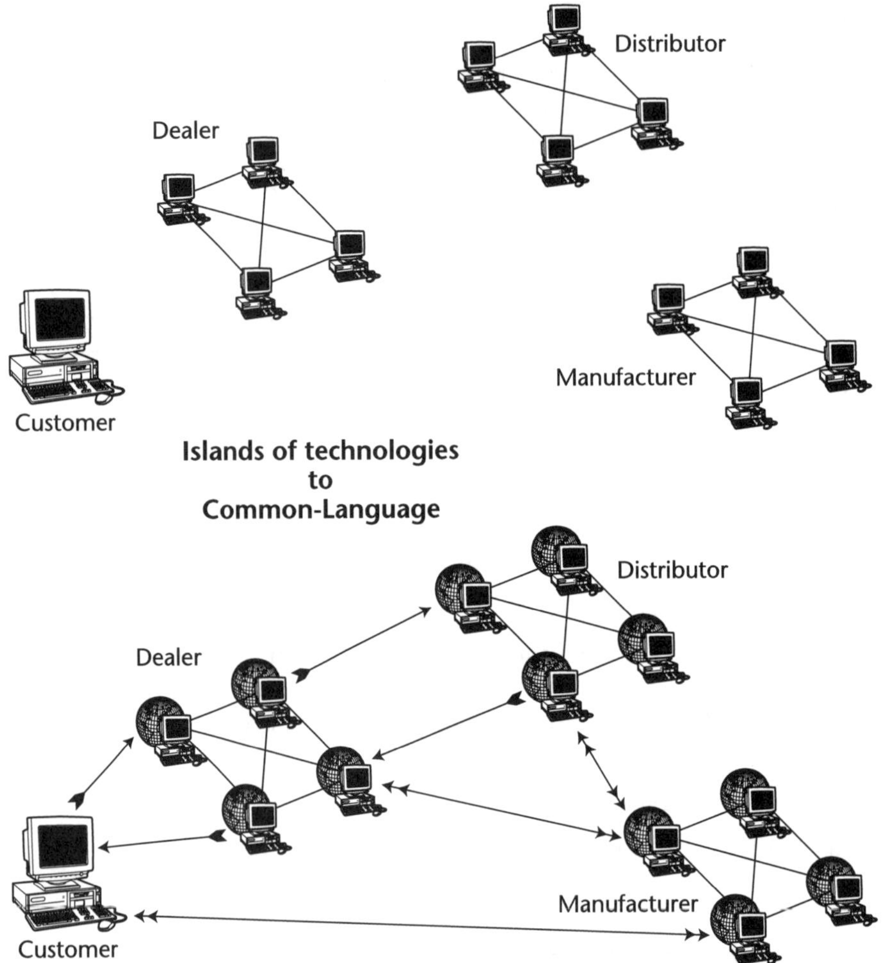

Figure 7.19 Islands of data and technology do not permit a "chain" in the supply chain.

The Problem

Trading partners experience a number of common problems; it is as if every trading partner speaks its own language and every transaction among trading partners requires labor to translate them.

- Major communications problems exist among trading partners
- Partners' computer systems may have different part numbers for the same items.
- There can be multiple sources of a product that fills the same need.

- The data structures among partners vary significantly.
- The data they must exchange (price, availability, configurations, documentation, and so on) is constantly changing.
- Many trading partners have identical problems keeping data current.

Providing an industry with a commercial library of products that is cross-referenced among its trading partners creates a Common-Language in which an industry can trade. Saabre is a commercial library for airplane seats that runs on a private network. Wine Operations, Inc, with the WineOps data set, is the Common-Language of the wine industry.

Providing affordable business software that is tailored to the Common-Language data sets creates Common-Tools. Trading partners do not have to invest labor to translate their transactions. The business systems of their partners can directly communicate, and a business-to- business (B2B) conduit is established.

The Concept of B2B Conduits

Special orders are normally a great problem for small businesses. They require labor to take the order, add the products to the business system, document the transaction, track progress, and support and deliver the goods or services. In addition to this added work is the tendency for customers to be so concerned about the order that they pester the retailer for the latest status.

One of the reasons for Amazon.com's excellent customer service rating is that it makes every order seem like it is precious. A second reason is that I can order whatever I need. Third, I can order it whenever I need it. Fourth, I can order at whatever time of day I recognize that I have a need. I love Amazon.com. Its handholding is excellent, automated but excellent.

I like the service so much that I translated Ingram Book's data into WebClerk to create the BookClerk data set. This permits every bookstore to behave like Amazon.com: The customer can see any title available and customer service is integrated. Customers can peruse special orders and browse the bookshelves for additional items.

Change

It is difficult to get change adopted, however. Desktop Hosting will be a major change in the way businesses manage unattended communications, and its initial adoption will likely take on the characteristics of other new high-tech business and technology concepts.

Crossing the Chasm is an excellent book by Moore and McKenna (1999) that explains why high-tech businesses can fail when developing markets for new technology. It uses the computer companies' failures in the mid-1980s to illustrate the time and sales gap—the chasm—that exists between early adopters of a technology and mainstream acceptance (Figure 7.20).

Change is driven by emotion. Some people love change and actively look for the next concept and take the next leap; others only implement change when the fear of being left behind overwhelms the fear of change. An emotional imperative to change is stimulated by appealing to some basic emotions:

Excite everyone's self-interest: I can sell more. I can service my customers better, at lower cost. I can market to customers using the Web as my own miniature television broadcasting station.

Excite fear: If I don't offer better unattended communications to my customers, my competitors will.

In the wine industry, change is stimulated based on certain rationale:

Consumers: I can demystify wine buying. I can read about wines, the vineyard, and even food and recipes the winery recommends with its wine. I can see awards and ratings. I can see what is in stock at my local retailer. I can place a special order for wine that my local retailer does not carry and still pick it up from my local store. I can send gifts via the WineOps' network and have it delivered by a local retailer.

Wineries: I can get my products known by many more customers and listed in many more retail outlets.

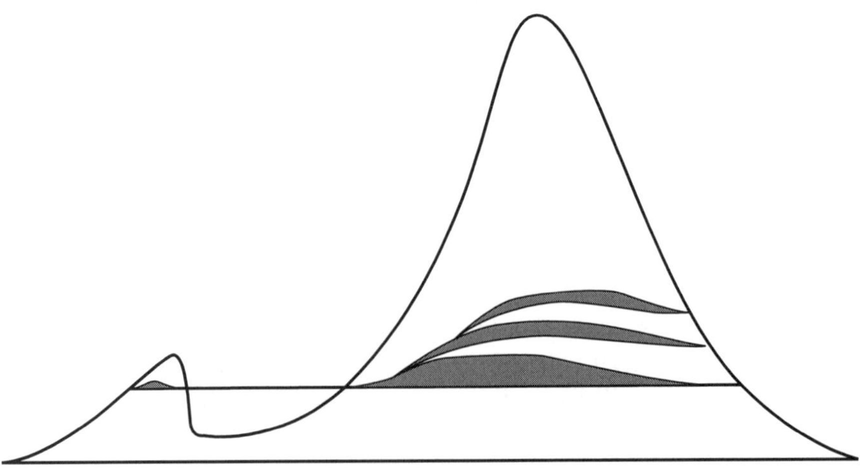

Figure 7.20 Time and sales gap between early and mainstream adoption of technology.

Wholesalers: I can show my inventory and buy from and sell directly to my customers and vendors.

Retailers: I can increase wine inventory turns, use email to market to my customers, provide product expertise, and automatically process special orders.

Profit Improvements in the Fine Wine Industry

Table 7.5 shows how a typical beverage retailer can increase profitable sales by adopting a just-in-time inventory model that is supported by the technology of Desktop Hosting. Similar cost reductions are expected for other retailers in other industries.

The primary improvement is the result of increasing the inventory turns of fine wine. Fine wines typically have the best margins, but slowest turns, so increasing sales of these items is noticeably profitable. The following summary is calculated from Table 7.5:

INCOME CHANGES		
Income	$30,400	From growth of GM ($)
Carry Savings	$64,389	Improvement in annual net carrying cost
	$94,789	
BALANCE SHEET CHANGES		
Capital Freed	**$357,715**	From reduced inventory on hand

Create the Technology, Data, and Training

The following components may be assembled to achieve the benefits of Desktop Hosting:

Common-Language. Drive out the complexities of maintaining constantly changing commercial data. Provide a library of wines and beverages that is superior to any that an individual company can afford to maintain on its own. Rent that data set to subscribers at a price that is less than the cost savings generated by use.

Common-Tools. Provide affordable business software that can use the Common-Language to run each subscriber's physical business: WebClerk, RetailClerk, and CommerceExpert.

B2B Conduits. Implement communications capabilities between trading partners so transactions can be posted into each other's business system without the cost of EDI (electronic data interchange), XML (extensible markup language), or any other translation technology. Reinforce existing trusted relationships with business and communications technologies.

Table 7.5 Profit Improvements Resulting from Higher Inventory Turns for Fine Wine*

TODAY

CATEGORY	SALES (%)	GM (%)	GM EFFECT (%)	GM ($)	YEAR ($)	SALES/ INVENTORY	YEARLY PO'S ($)	TURNS	ON HAND	NET CARRYING COST/YEAR ($)
Beer/Beverages	35	12	4	168,000	1,400,000	5%	1,232,000	25	49,280	8,870
Premium Beer	5	25	1	50,000	200,000	5%	150,000	3	50,000	9,000
Spirits	30	18	5	216,000	1,200,000	25%	984,000	4	246,000	44,280
Premium Spirits	5	25	1	50,000	200,000	10%	150,000	1.5	100,000	18,000
Wines	20	28	6	224,000	800,000	25%	576,000	2.3	250,435	45,078
Premium Wines	5	40	2	80,000	200,000	30%	120,000	0.4	300,000	54,000
TOTAL	**100**		**20**	**788,000**	**4,000,000**	**100%**	**3,212,000**		**995,715**	**179,229**

CHANGE AFTER ONE YEAR OF USING DESKTOP HOSTING CONCEPTS

CATEGORY	SALES (%)	GM (%)	GM EFFECT (%)	GM ($)	YEAR ($)	SALES/ INVENTORY	YEARLY PO'S ($)	TURNS	ON HAND	NET CARRYING COST/YEAR ($)
Beer/Beverages	34	12	4	168,000	1,400,000	5%	1,232,000	25.0	49,280	8,870
Premium Beer	5	25	1	50,000	200,000	5%	150,000	3.0	50,000	9,000
Spirits	29	18	5	216,000	1,200,000	25%	984,000	4.0	246,000	44,280
Premium Spirits	5	25	1	50,000	200,000	10%	150,000	1.5	100,000	18,000
Wines	21	28	6	246,400	880,000	25%	633,600	*5.0*	*126,720*	22,810
Premium Wines	5	40	2	88,000	220,000	30%	132,000	*2.0*	*66,000*	11,880
TOTAL	**100**		**20%**	**818,400**	**4,100,000**	**100%**	**3,281,600**		**638,000**	**114,840**

*Details in Table 7.5 were developed by Kjell Adstedt for WineOps based on interviews with wine retailers.

Virtual-Inventory. Drive down inventory carrying costs, free-up capital, and expand product offerings.

Desktop Hosting. Define the benefits of networking unattended communications.

Create the Example of How to Win

The following actions define the approach for implementing Desktop Hosting in the fine wine industry:

Find the early adopters and seed them with some support. Early adopters are only 1 to 2 percent of the market, but they account for 100 percent of the sample that mainstream companies will emulate.

Drive the cost to implement toward zero. The software and data can be obtained from www.wineops.com

Drive out the technical complexities and uncertainties. As shown on the Services page (Figure 7.21) from the WineOps Web site, WineOps offers a complete suite of:

- Business software
- Data libraries
- Computer and network hardware
- Internet, network, and wireless communications services
- Training, marketing support, technical support, and other services

Empowering Profit Centers

General Needs: Sales is the most vital process in every for-profit company. We have developed enterprise software to manage this selling process from the marketing effort to the check clearing the bank.

JITCorp had to create two distinct products because of the difference between the selling process of retailers (business to consumers, or B2C) and manufacturers/wholesalers (business to business, or B2B). Those products are:

RetailClerk. Point-of-sale and enterprise software for retailers (B2C).

CommerceExpert. Enterprise software for manufacturers, distributors, wholesalers, and independent sales representatives (B2B). Figure 7.22 illustrates the flow in the sales process from marketing effort to the check in the bank.

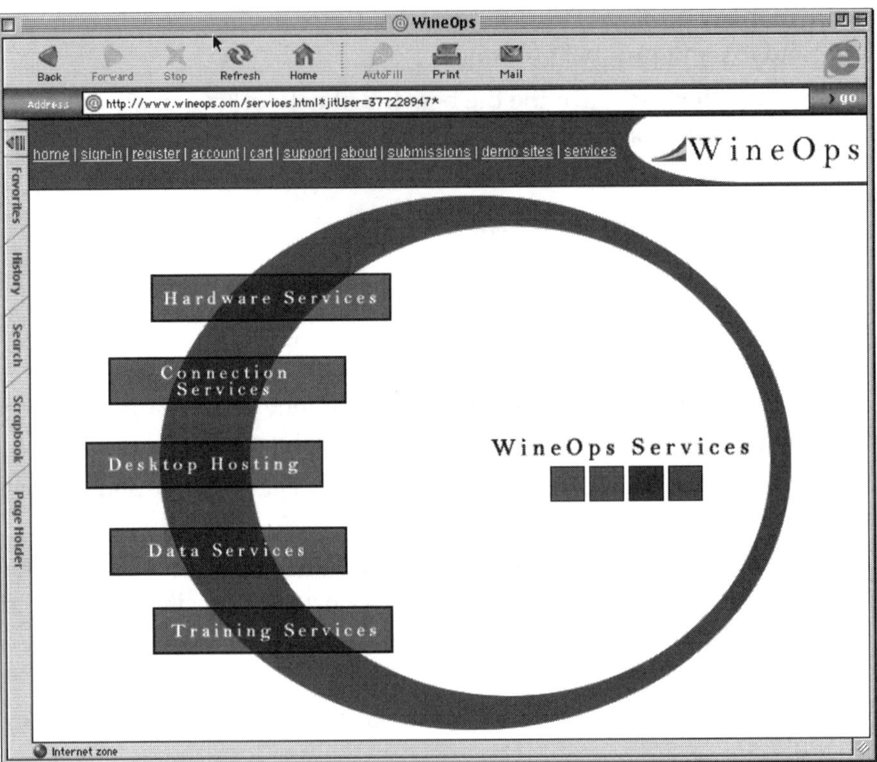

Figure 7.21 The www.WineOps.com Services page shows the breadth of services that can be offered to support the Desktop Hosting concept in the fine wine industry.

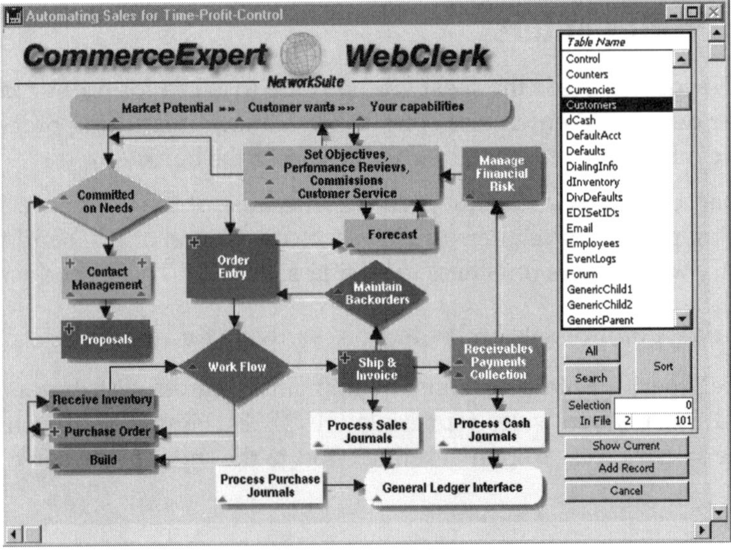

Figure 7.22 Flow of the sales process.

Small companies use the software products to run their entire company. Large companies use the products to run each of their profit centers. This empowering of profit centers is different from most enterprise software solutions. Most solutions are top-down, where the entire enterprise is treated as a single entity. Our approach is to look at a large company as a collection of profit centers. We empower each profit center, tailor the solution to the special needs of each profit center, and then collect their individual efforts into the company's general ledger. This bubble-up approach of empowering profit centers has several benefits:

- The selling process remains the first priority of the profit center, and the technology, data, and training are made to assist in attaining that goal.
- Accountability is enhanced as transactions among profit centers document actual resource consumption instead of overheads being allocated by departments.
- ROP (return on pain) is enhanced. The team that must live with the solution is in control of it and can tailor it to its benefit.
- The gigantic task of automating a large company is broken into bite-size pieces.
- Companies can buy, sell, create, and eliminate profit centers without the pain of integrating with or separating from a large enterprise system. This permits profit center information to stand alone and then use the network to submit aggregated data into the general ledger. It also permits easier tailoring of the distributed systems to take advantage of changing market conditions.
- The advantage for WineOps and JITCorp is that this approach is easily applied to the automation of entire supply chains. Conceptually, entire industries are simply a series of profit centers that benefit from enhancing their selling process and integrating their unattended communications. RetailClerk, CommerceExpert, and WebClerk combine to create JITCorp's SupplyChainSuite. WineOps is licensed by JITCorp to deliver this technology to the beverage industry.

Security: SSL connection, VPN (virtual private network), and other security needs are easily established depending on the requirements of the trading partners.

Hardware: This uses a standard network with typical computers. In addition, the following discussion describes our current experience with handheld devices and other potential wireless solutions. This is a high-level summary of the state of the art in early 2002. This is an area of rapid change, so always check for current information from technology suppliers or Web sites.

We have experience with iPAQ Windows CE palm devices, officially known as the Microsoft Windows Powered iPAQ Pocket PC. These devices create a remote controller back to WebClerk. We use these in three configurations and foresee a possible fourth:

Wireless network inside a store. We set up a IEEE 802.11b-compliant network. The specific devices we have used are Apple's AirPort for the hub with Lucent and Sony PC cards. It is very important to confirm there are iPAQ or other CE device drivers before you buy any of the PC cards.

This allows store clerks to access the company's product offerings from its iPAQ anywhere in the store. When combined with a barcode scanner, employees can answer questions about any product by simply scanning its bar code. The barcode PC card we have used is made by Socket. Other solutions are available and may suit your needs.

These Pocket PCs can even be used as overload cash registers. They can ring up a sale and place it as a Web order. This order then displays as a pending order on the cash register. The cash register is used to clear the transaction and handle the money.

Wireless network via cell phone. Using the Wireless Web Card from Targus and a Motorola TimePort, the iPAQ has the same capabilities to control a Desktop Hosting machine. This combination is limited to 19 kilobytes per second (kbps). It's not perfect, but it does give access to customer information anywhere that is supported by the cell phone provider.

Wireless network. Sprint's AirCard 510 permits the iPAQ to have full capabilities to control a Desktop Hosting machine. It is limited to the areas serviced by Sprint. Other solutions are available and in development.

Ricochet is a fourth possible configuration. Ricochet is in Chapter 11 liquidation, but if this network revives, it will be a useful tool for those who must access the details in their business system while on the road.

Communications: Digital connectivity to the Internet is required. For most businesses, a DSL line is adequate. DSL, ISDN, frame relay, T1, and other connections are all good choices. It is possible to get by with a nailed-up analog connection if no other economically reasonable choice is available. Bandwidth of greater than 128 kbps is desired; 56 kbps is an absolute minimum.

Software: Intranets are client/server configurations run by CommerceExpert for wineries and distributors. Retailers use RetailClerk. WebClerk provides the extranet capabilities. It needs to have a separate jitWebCE folder with pages specifically designed to fit the limited display of an iPAQ.

Learning Exercises

B2B Conduits

1. Launch the WebClerk application.
2. Click on the Launch WebClerk button.
3. Close the WebClerk Flow and TechNotes windows.
4. Go to the Ord menu and select Search by Order#. A dialog will open.
5. Type in 2120.
6. Click on OK. Order 2120 will display. This is the order placed in Case Study 6. We need to order the wine for this event.
7. Go to the Navigation Pallet (upper-left corner). Click on the General pop-up, drag down to the Inv/POs page, and release the mouse button.
8. Highlight the two wine line items, Firstland's Sauvignon Blanc and Cabernet Sauvignon line items.
9. Click on the + side of the Add/Change PO button in the lower left of the screen. A dialog window will open asking you to add a new PO or add to an existing PO.

NOTE

The Add/Change buttons in the program all have a + and a triangle or delta. Delta is the mathematical symbol for change.

10. Click on the OK button to add a new PO. The PO screen will open with the line item added at your cost.
11. Type Comm and press the tab key. The cursor was on the name of the vendor company. The program will search for that vendor and return the U.S. importer of Firstland products, Commandeur.
12. This next step is not required, but it helps to understand what is happening. Go to the Navigation Pallet. Click on General, drag to Vendor/Ship, and release the mouse. The vendor page will display.

    The Domain entry is in the left center of the screen and the User/Pass entries are below it. The screen shows the B2B Conduit page at the vendor's Web site and your username and password at that site.
    In this demo, it actually points to your own machine 127.0.0.1; therefore, this will be posted right back to you.
13. On this page and the General page is a small graphic of a clipboard. Click on the clipboard. You will be asked if you wish to place a WebPO. Click on OK.
14. If your operating system is set up to know which browser you use, it will launch and a Web page will display.

NOTE

If this does not happen, you will need to launch your browser and type in http://127.0.0.1/b2bconduit.htm and click on the Enter key.

15. Click on the large entry area. Enter Control-V or Command-V to paste in the contents of the clipboard. Your purchase order will display in a B2B format.
16. Click Post and your purchase order will be posted into the vendor's quote system. Because it posted to your own machine, when you sign in with username Terra and password Terra, you will see the proposal. It is intended that vendors will review posted requests before they are processed into firm orders.

Purchasing with Desktop Hosting

This exercise demonstrates uses of the Web from a buyer's point of view.

1. Go to the WebClerk application splash screen.
2. Go to the Dept menu >> Production. The window will change to the Production Department splash screen.
3. Go to POs menu >> Show Open POs. The open purchase order will display. Note the values in the Vendor Status column on the right side of the window. At the bottom of this window is a WebStatus button, which will cause your computer to connect with all your vendors' WebClerk-compliant Web servers and update the status of your purchase orders based on the values in their sales orders (Figure 7.23).

In this exercise, PO 15 points to your WebClerk as the vendor's Web server. This purchase order is tied to the sales order 2015. If you change the [Orders]StatusCustomer value in the sales order and repeat this exercise, you will see the value of the purchase order status change.

If a buyer needs to act on any specific order:

1. Open the Input Layout of the purchase order.
2. Click on the Domain label in the window. This will launch your browser and open the vendor's Web site.
3. Sign-in at the vendor's site.
4. Click on Status URL to show open orders.
5. Click on the URL for order 2015. This will display the full order. At the bottom of the page is a service request.
6. Fill out the service request asking to increase the order quantity for item 100033 to 3.

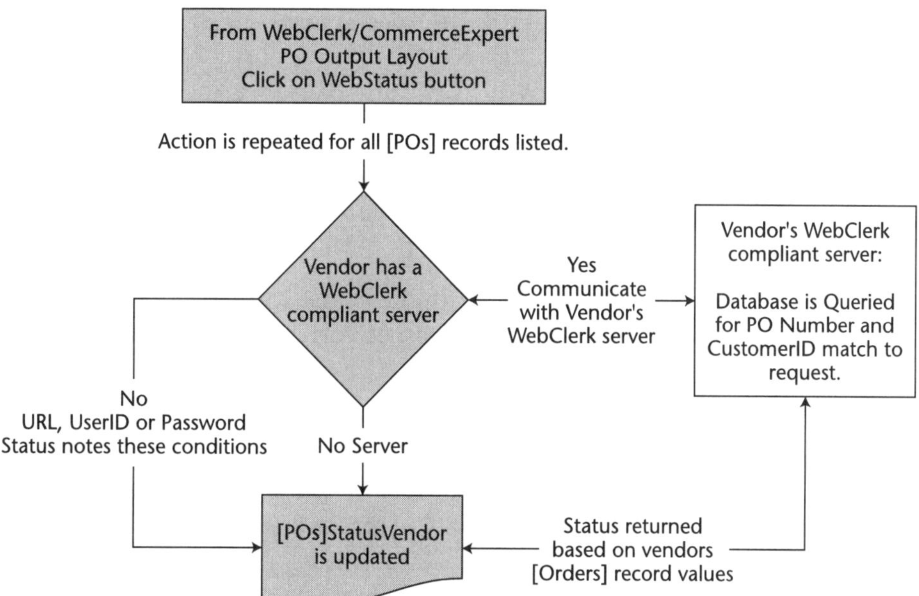

Figure 7.23 Desktop Hosting between a buyer's desk and the vendor's sales desk.

7. Go back to your WebClerk application.
8. Go to the Sales splash screen.
9. Go to the Search By Order#. A dialog window will open for entering the order you wish to see.
10. Enter 2015 and click on OK. Order 2015 will display.
11. Go to the Navigation Pallet, click and hold on General and drag down to Shipping. The Shipping page will display.
12. Press Control-R or Command-R, or go to the Actions menu and drag down to Related Files (depending on default settings, this step may not be required). The [Service] record you submitted via the Web will display in the bottom-left portion of the screen.
13. Double-click on the [Service] record to display the full record.

This demonstrates how a buyer can communicate changes to the vendor's sales order. The request is not an email that might get lost, missed, or forgotten. The change goes directly into the vendor's corporate memory. If you make the changes requested to the sales order, go back to your browser and call up the sales order again, you will find that either the order has been adjusted to reflect the request or the pending [Service] record is still active.

As an alternative, go back to the Sales splash screen and go to the Review menu >> Pending Service Records. The [Service] record will display in the list of pending actions. Review the Learning Exercises and movies on the CD for more details on managing customer service.

This exercise may be a little confusing because your machine is acting as both the customer and the vendor. The benefit is that you can view the entire flow of interactive communications.

Many more features and opportunities exist to further extend the networks between companies. The value of a network expands geometrically with the number of active interconnected nodes. Figure 7.24 shows how network configurations have evolved.

Many companies currently have their internal and the external networks separated. Like a manual switchboard, labor must be invested at every connection. The value of the Internet will be realized as Desktop Hosting computers automatically connect business relationships. Again, this puts the point of communication at the point of action.

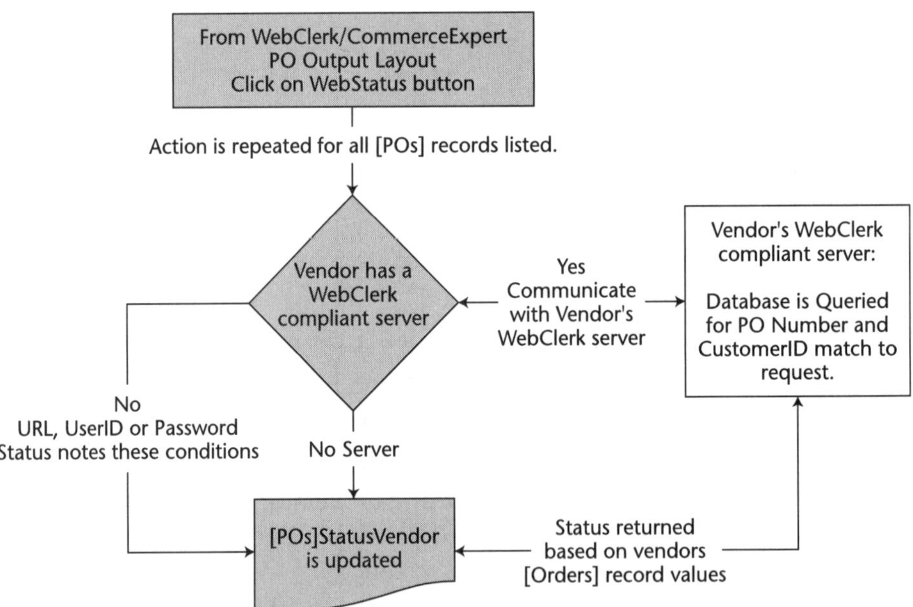

Figure 7.24 Network evolution to publish-based unattended communications results in the network becoming more and more valuable.

Summary

As Desktop Hosting expands, a business will be no more likely to have a single e-commerce site than it would run an entire company with a single telephone. Companies will empower each point of action to communicate directly with the trading partners that are essential to their requirements for adding value or controlling costs. Typical interactions include:

- Purchasing agents will work with vendors from their desktops.
- Salespeople will work with customers from their desktops.
- Marketing will work with PR firms from their desktops.

Instead of the sneaker net between the intranets and extranets, there will be protected but direct access among the business systems of trading partners. The number of active connected points in the network will mushroom and Kelly's Prime Law of Networks will apply:

> *Value explodes exponentially with membership, while this value explosion sucks in yet more members. The virtuous circle inflates until all potential members are joined.*
>
> Kevin Kelly—"New Rules for the New Economy," *Wired* magazine, September 1997

Networks will evolve from labor-intensive, email-message–based sneaker nets to interactive publishing nodes putting the point of communications at the point of action.

Case Study 8: Schools and Noncommercial Desktop Hosting

By empowering everyone and focusing on different interest groups, Desktop Hosting enables schools and noncommercial organizations to automate at a price they can afford.

Specification

Objective: Improve the ability to communicate and coordinate the interest of schools, interest groups, their community, and alumni. Figure 7.25 shows how different groups within a school system can use the network and Desktop Hosting to advantage.

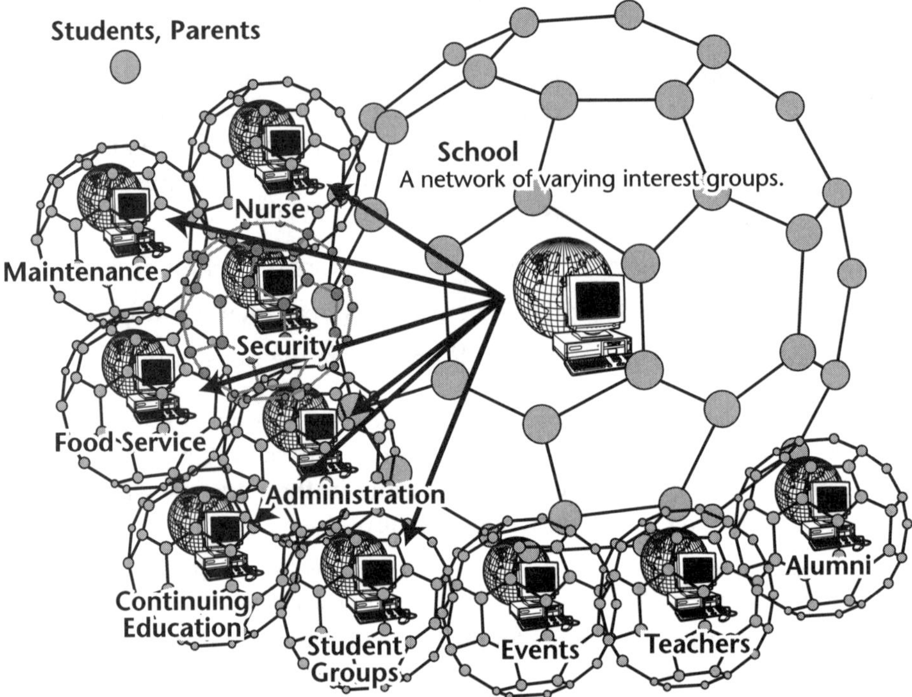

Figure 7.25 The network of varying interest groups associated with schools.

Points of Interest: Like the hotel example (Case Study 6), schools have many interest groups that have different relationships with their members than with the school as a whole. Empowering each node with its own Desktop Hosting server tailors the solution to the need.

Examples are provided for:

- Teacher, student, parent networks
- Events: plays, concerts, sporting
- Bookstore
- Alumni groups

Concerns:

- The system needs to be secure so that only authorized people can make modifications to the site.
- Personal information needs to be secure.
- The tendency to overprotect or restrict communications tools for fear of abuse must be kept in check.

Lessons:

1. Experience is more important than age.

   Students today have more experience on the Web than most adults. Teenagers significantly contributed to most of the Web examples in this book. Given guidance, then freedom to act, anyone can achieve an education that is relevant, timely, interesting, and profitable.

   Sites like www.WebClerk.com, www.WineOps.com, and www.PizzaClerk.com were all built by high school students. They all received pay and stock for their efforts. The SEGA example (Case Study 4) was implemented by a 17-year-old.

2. Teaching Desktop Hosting is not very well suited to classic classroom time. It is like building skills in music, athletics, or computer games. It seems more a development than learning process. There are three phases to internalizing Desktop Hosting:

Mill-around-time. This is typically the time when most learners give up. The tasks required to build and manage the Web are repetitive. Seeing the repetitive pattern requires a "soak time." Like computer games, music, or athletics, long and concentrated hours are spent probing and experimenting to find and load the environment into the player's head.

Tunnel-through. Again, concentrated hours are spent repeating the identified patterns to build skills. It is as if there is a mountain range between beginners and performers. It is too tall to climb and too far to walk around. Getting through this phase is a head-down, tunnel-through event. For musical instruments, this is the time when you know the keys to press, but the music mostly squawks. The only way through is extended and concentrated practice.

Performance. This is the fun phase. The patterns are loaded into people's heads, and they can execute. This is also the phase in which individuals begin forming teams and skills begin to specialize. In our office, Mike Cassano and Bryan Wedel started when they were about 16. Mike has become a master of data manipulation; Bryan's artwork is spectacular. They know the spectrum of fundamentals, so they can concentrate their individual efforts while assuring a seamless integration of their efforts.

Table 7.6 shows a list of recommended tools. They are not required, but this list is provided based on what works for us. You are invited to participate in the forums at www.DesktopHosting.com to distribute ideas on tools, teaching, and techniques. Manufacturers are encouraged to list their products and the functions they provide.

Table 7.6 Software Tools that Manage Desktop Hosting Sites

TOOL	PURPOSE	MANUFACTURER
WebClerk	Database and Webserver	JITCorp
BBEdit	Text and HTML editor (Mac)	Bare Bones Software
EditPlus	Text and HTML editor (Win)	ES-Computing
Dreamweaver	WYSIWYG HTML editor	MacroMedia
Photoshop	Image editor	Adobe
Flash	Animated vector movies	MacroMedia
Premier	Video editing	Adobe
QuickTime	Plug-in for playing movies	Apple
CameraMan	Captures computer screen into movies	Motion Works International, Inc.
Snapz Pro		Ambrosia Software, Inc.
MediaCleaner	Optimizes movies for cross platform, Web and CD	Terran Interactive
Word	Checks text for spelling and grammar	Microsoft
Internet Explorer	Web browser	Microsoft
Navigator		Netscape

General Needs: Manage communications at many different nodes with diverse interests.

Security: There may be a need to provide secure financial transactions in bookstores and for continuing education, registration, and other similar activities. There is a need to have multiple points of secured access to the same records; an example is parents and children who may see common files. Physical security for individual servers needs to be provided so that unattended teacher networks can be managed by creative students.

Hardware: Hardware required is consistent with what is typically available in schools.

Software: The examples use WebClerk as a server. This software is not specifically tailored to all the examples provided. WebClerk is used because it is what comes with this book. Other relationship-serving software that more precisely meet the needs discussed are likely to be fielded by various creators.

Learning Exercises

Teacher, Student, Parent Network

Teachers have limited time to call or meet with every parent during the school year. But in the course of documenting their students' efforts, they can build a communications network with the parents. This is an example of creating an unattended network centered on the teacher with access to a student and that student's mom, dad, or grandparent. An active relationship among the parents, teacher, and student can help keep a student focused on achieving the desired goals. We will look first at the teacher's database side of the network and then at the same information displayed via the Web to the parents and student.

1. Go to the WebClerk application. Close out all windows so that the Sales splash screen is showing (click on OK or X in the Navigation Pallet, upper left of open windows).
2. Go to the Customer menu >> Find Customer. A dialog window will open.
3. In the Name field enter Jam,Ko. This is part of the last name, a comma and part of a first name. There are no spaces.
4. Hit the Tab or Return key to initiate a search. One record will display in the list below.
5. Double-click on the record in the list to display the child's record. In the bottom of the window, a list of active service records is displayed. These records are examples of on-going communications between parents and students. The publish levels of some of these records limit access so that parents can see information not typically available to a student.

NOTE

In the event the autorelate feature has been deactivated, the list of active service records will display if you enter Control-R (or Command-R for Mac users).

6. Click on the R check box on the right center of the Customers - General screen. A list of four RemoteUsers is displayed. These represent the student, individual parents, and a grandparent for the child. When finished viewing these records, click on the OK button at the bottom of the Output Layout to return to the Customer record.

   View the RemoteUser records by double-clicking on any desired record. Authority levels can be set differently for different RemoteUsers. In the case of the parents, the authority level is set higher. This allows the teacher to make records available to the parents that are not visible to the student.

7. From the Customer record, General page, view any of the Service records at the bottom of the layout by double-clicking on them. Close out of any record entered by clicking once on the OK or X buttons in the Navigation Pallet in the upper left of the window.

NOTE

It is possible to add, delete, modify, complete, publish, and unpublish these records. Review the training movies and exercises on the CD that accompanies this book.

8. Confirm that your WebClerk is serving the Web.
9. Launch a browser and go to address http://localhost
10. Click on the Sign-In URL to display the sign-in page. This can also be a secured entry page so that the username and password are encrypted while transferring over the Web.

    Enter username Mom and password Mother. Click on the Submit button. The student's record will display. View any desired record. It is possible to give parents the ability to add new Service Records.

    Repeat for username Dad and password Father, username Student and password Kid.
11. In the browser, go to http://localhost/teacher.html. This displays a sample home page for a teacher to communication with parents and students.

Events: Plays, Concerts, Sporting Events

This example shows how database records can be used to create interactive Web sites.

1. In a browser, go to http://localhost/Events.html to display a list of events at a school. This is a frame-creation page that will display the Events_Index.html (left side) and Events_Display.html (right side) pages.
2. In the left frame, click on the sky-diving event. The WebClerk database is queried, and a record is displayed on the right side. This is an example of how a record might look before an event. In the next section we will add pictures of the event to the record.
3. Go to the WebClerk application. Close out all windows until only a splash screen is showing (Click on OK or X in the Navigation Pallet, upper left of open windows).
4. Go to the Action menu >> Search. A dialog window will open.
5. A pop-up list of the database tables is just below the Navigation Pallet (upper left of the window). Click on this list and drag down to and release on the TallyResults table. The fields for this table will display in the list below the pop-up.

6. A list of standard queries for this table is on the right side of the layout. Click once on the Events query under the Name header to display the bottom of the screen. Click on the Execute button or double-click on Events query to execute a search and display the resulting records.
7. Double-click on the sky-dive event. The date, time, and other specifics for the event are provided in the record.
8. Go to the File menu >> Print Defined Report. A dialog of standard reports is displayed. Double-click on the Post Pictures report. A dialog window will open asking you to Select a folder to post graphics from.
9. Navigate to the Skydive folder. The typical path for a Windows-based PC is C:\WebClerk\jitWeb\images\Skydive.
   - When you select this folder, the standard report executes.
   - The path to the images and to a thumbnail of these images is added to the TallyResult record that documents the event.
   - The TallyResults record is saved.
   - Students would normally capture these images, post them to a folder like the one provided, and make the thumbnail images.
10. Return to the browser and click on the sky-dive event again (you may need to Refresh or Reload the page). You will see the contents that were in the TallyResults record. It has been amended to display the graphics that were captured of the event.

NOTE

This is a simple example. It can be extended to include video, updating scores, running commentary, and so forth. Set the imaginations of your students loose.

Look at the reservation capabilities to see how events and commercial actions can be related.

This same technique can be applied to an ever-expanding online yearbook.

Bookstore

Other case studies show how commercial activities use Desktop Hosting. The bookstore example is provided in overview only to emphasize that even schools have a commercial aspect and can service that aspect.

1. With WebClerk running and its Web-serving capability turned on, go to your browser.
2. Go to http://localhost/bookstore.html. A page will display. Click on various computer options to see how a school's bookstore can process orders.

Figure 7.26 An alumni Web site.

Alumni

Keeping in touch with classmates is valuable on many levels. Schools can be rallying points. Here is a quick example of how to stay in contact with member of a alumni network (see Figure 7.26). Database records drive this site. By looking at the URLs, you can see which table is queried and see the results of such queries displayed in a browser.

1. With WebClerk running and its Web-serving capability turned on, go to your browser.
2. Go to http://localhost/alumni.html. A page will display. Click on various computer options to see various features. Look at the URLs and then go to the WebClerk database and search for the matching records.

Summary

Unattended communications are not limited to business transactions. They can be extended to many aspects of relationships and transactions—commercial or not—that can benefit from communicating a shared objective.

PART THREE

Getting Started with the Programs

CHAPTER 8

Using the Tools

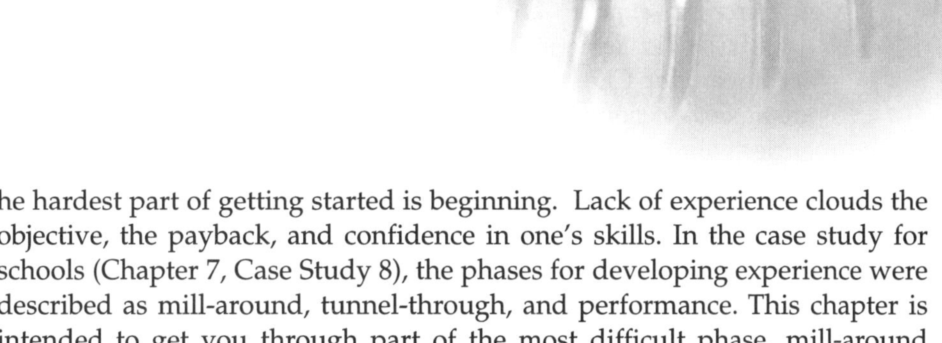

The hardest part of getting started is beginning. Lack of experience clouds the objective, the payback, and confidence in one's skills. In the case study for schools (Chapter 7, Case Study 8), the phases for developing experience were described as mill-around, tunnel-through, and performance. This chapter is intended to get you through part of the most difficult phase, mill-around effort, and it covers:

- Where you can find more training support via the Web, Commerce-Expert.pdf, TechNotes, and movies
- The WebClerk/CommerceExpert applications
- Preliminary activities required for running the WebClerk application
- Installing the application
- Layouts in the application and how the program looks
- Navigating the application
- Customizing the application to your needs

More Training Support

More training support is provided from several electronic sources (Web sites, files on the CD, and interactive notes within the application), and in the appendixes on the accompanying CD-ROM:

www.DesktopHosting.com. This Web site has forums for sharing ideas, problems, and solutions with others. This is a general site that covers products beyond WebClerk. Individuals and companies are encouraged to list their products and ideas at this site.

www.WebClerk.com. This Web site has a list of available training seminars for WebClerk/CommerceExpert users, plus forums and interactive online help. This is a commercial site supporting the WebClerk/CommerceExpert and other JITCorp products and services.

CommerceExpert.pdf. This is an Adobe Acrobat document that details the flowcharts displayed in Appendixes A and B (all are included on the accompanying CD). Figure 8.1 shows that on the right of the opening page are links to various training categories. Clicking on any one of these categories will display a list of movies with a brief explanation of each.

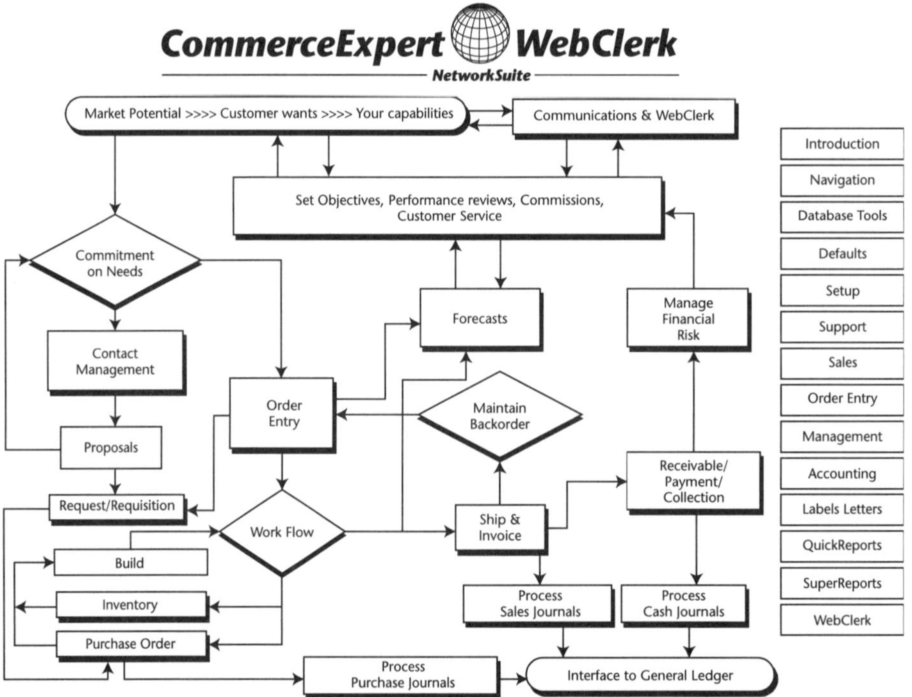

Figure 8.1 Select links within CommerceExpert.pdf to play training movies.

TechNotes

TechNotes is the Help area of WebClerk/CommerceExpert; it contains searchable help, training movies, and technical notes. The interactive documentation is presented via this mechanism because it is cross-platform, running on both PCs and Macintosh computers. Although TechNotes are typically used by those running the WebClerk software on their desktops, the text of TechNotes can be displayed on the Web site as well.

General Information

TechNotes are in the demo data set that comes with this CD. When WebClerk is first launched, the TechNotes window is set to automatically open and display the TechNotes with the subject Startup (Figure 8.2 shows the layout for this subject). Reading these notes is very helpful. The list of movies provides links and descriptions for the 150 movies on the enclosed CD. You can print TechNotes by highlighting the desired TechNote in the list at the right side of the TechNote Window and clicking on the Print button.

Like any other field with a bold label, the entry boxes for **Chapter**, **Name**, **Subject**, and **Keyword** will perform a search on that particular item. The **Body** is all hyperlinked, and clicking on any word in the body will execute a search for other TechNotes with that as the key word. You can disable this hyperlinked activity over on the left-hand side by turning off the HYPER TEXT check box. If you have difficulty finding a TechNote and want to mark its location, you can add a key word to it by clicking the Key button and entering your word into the Keyword area; it will add your word to the Keyword collection.

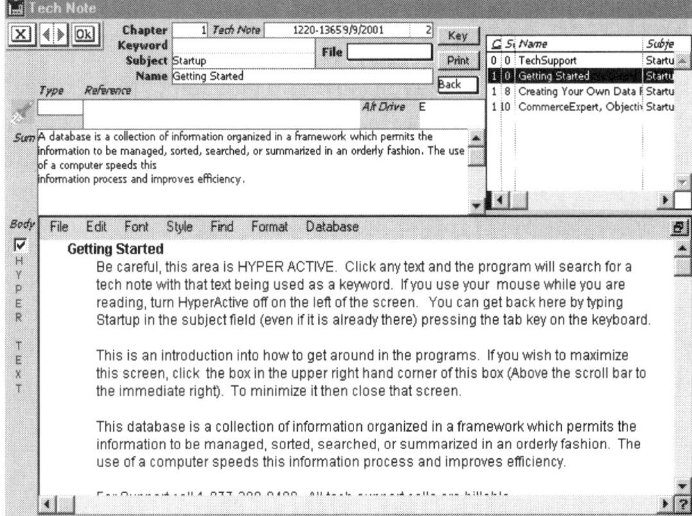

Figure 8.2 Layout for the TechNotes online interactive technical documentation.

On the enclosed CD, the movie i7_TechS.MOV is a helpful overview of how the TechNotes work.

NOTE

People who have been using Microsoft Windows software for a long time will need to spend a little time getting comfortable with the way TechNotes are assembled and presented. If the Tech Note window is not already on your screen, select the Depts menu and pull down Tech Note Reference. Figure 8.2 shows the general layout of how Tech Notes are presented.

NOTE

On a PC, make sure to put the letter drive of the CD into the Alt Drive field (in the top, right of middle of the screen) shown in Figure 8.3.

Learning Exercises

In TechNotes, enter Learning Exercises in the Subject field and press the Tab or Enter key. A list of learning exercises will display. Select the desired lesson by clicking on the list to the right of the screen. These are step-by-step lessons on various aspects of the application.

QuickSteps

In the TechNotes, enter QuickSteps in the Subject field and press the Tab or Enter key. A list of learning exercises will display. Select the desired lesson by clicking on the list to the right of the screen.

Movies on the Enclosed CD

Movies are an integral part of how we train. You can select them directly from the CD, but they are also available to launch from within the WebClerk TechNote area. Movies are typically played directly from the CD, so confirm that the WebClerk CD is in your desktop CD player.

In the Movies folder there are approximately 150 QuickTime movies on how to use the application. These are most easily accessed from the CommerceExpert.pdf file on the CD or from the TechNotes window. In TechNotes go to Keyword, type Movies, and then press the Tab or Enter key. The list of movies with a short description will display.

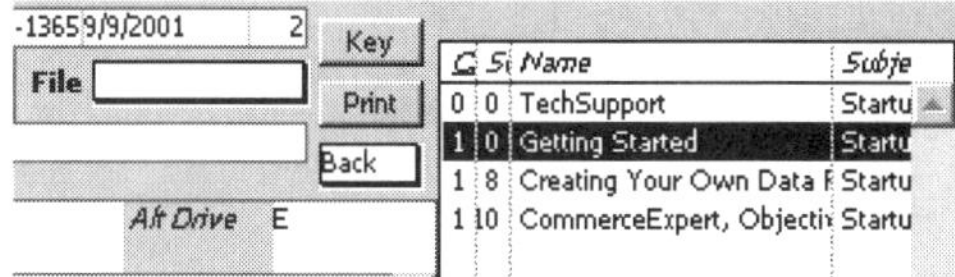

Figure 8.3 Location of the *Alt Drive* field in the WebClerk TechNotes (Windows users only).

If the Tech Note window is not already on your screen, select the Depts menu and pull down Tech Note Reference. You can click on any of the TechNotes, and in some of these notes will be a LaunchThis line, such as:

```
LaunchThis<-S15614:movies:i0_movie.MOV->
```

This launches the file into a helper application determined by the filename extension. In this case, it ends with MOV, so it will launch a movie (i0_movie.MOV) into your QuickTime Player.

NOTE

The first time you launch any document you will be asked to choose the application to run the document. Mac users should choose Movie Player or other QuickTime player; Windows users should select Player, Player32 (generally stored in the main drive in the Windows or WinNT folder) or other QuickTime player. It needs to be installed and active on your computer.

You will need to have QuickTime installed to play these movies. You can obtain a free download from Apple Computer at www.apple.com/quicktime/. These movies will play on PC or Macintosh computers.

NOTE

Microsoft Windows users: Put the letter value of your CD drive (Examples: D, E, F) into the *Alt Drive* field at the top of the Tech References layout). See the middle of Figure 8.3.

What Is WebClerk/CommerceExpert?

CommerceExpert is a database application that combines data structures, business logic, and intranet networking capabilities. It is a full-featured business enterprise sales and operations (ESO) management application that runs on either a Mac or PC platform. The objective of this software is to increase a customer's profitable sales. Profit is defined as the difference between the value that customers pay for and the cost to compete.

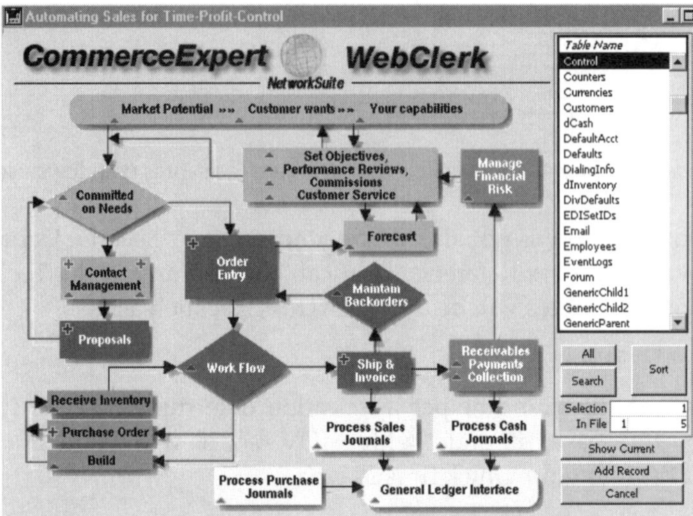

Figure 8.4 WebClerk/CommerceExpert supports the sales flow of an organization.

Selling is the most vital process in any for-profit company. Yet in most companies the technology supporting sales is a patchwork: contact management to generate activity, various word-processing templates and spreadsheets to manage marketing and proposals, some database or accounting program to manage orders, a different database to manage production and purchasing, and accounting software to invoice and collect receivables. Enterprise sales and operations (ESO) software integrates the entire selling process into a flow from the marketing effort to the "check to the bank."

CommerceExpert creates a flow for the selling process (Figure 8.4). From the marketing effort to the check clearing the bank, the entire selling process is integrated into the flow by the application. Communications is an integral part of the commerce engine. It is the aspect of leadership that makes trading partners aware of the value of their relationship with your company. This application is provided in either single-user (a full version is on the enclosed CD) or in client/server configurations.

WebClerk is the application that serves many of the CommerceExpert capabilities to the Internet. Its features tend to dominate use in the single-user configuration; therefore, the single-user version is generally referred to as WebClerk.

Layers to the Applications

The different logical layers of the applications are described in Figure 8.5.

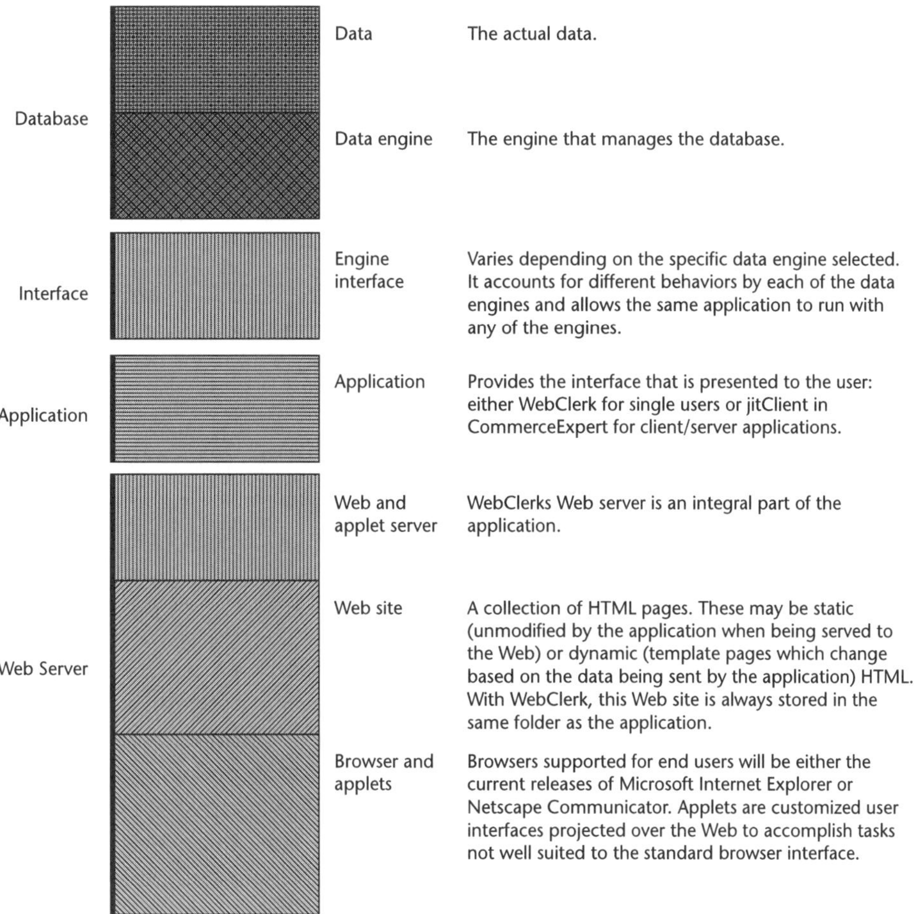

Database
Data
The actual data.
Data engine
The engine that manages the database.
Interface
Engine interface
Varies depending on the specific data engine selected. It accounts for different behaviors by each of the data engines and allows the same application to run with any of the engines.
Application
Application
Provides the interface that is presented to the user: either WebClerk for single users or jitClient in CommerceExpert for client/server applications.
Web Server
Web and applet server
WebClerks Web server is an integral part of the application.
Web site
A collection of HTML pages. These may be static (unmodified by the application when being served to the Web) or dynamic (template pages which change based on the data being sent by the application) HTML. With WebClerk, this Web site is always stored in the same folder as the application.
Browser and applets
Browsers supported for end users will be either the current releases of Microsoft Internet Explorer or Netscape Communicator. Applets are customized user interfaces projected over the Web to accomplish tasks not well suited to the standard browser interface.

Figure 8.5 Relationships among different logical layers of the WebClerk system.

Getting Ready: Preliminary Activities

The following sections walk through an overview of network connectivity requirements and describe a few graphics files that will be needed to customize your site. It is helpful to have these in place before installation, customization, and use of the WebClerk product, although they can be done in parallel.

Network Connectivity

It is assumed that the user has already worked with a local Internet Service Provider (ISP) to:

- Establish network connectivity to the Internet
- Obtain a fixed (permanent) TCP/IP address (this is like a fixed phone number to your computer)
- Map a domain name to that TCP/IP address via Domain Name Services (DNS). You can get your domain name from various sources. We typically use www.dotster.com or www.netsol.com.

It is also possible to do all the setup, configuration, and testing on a standalone machine, with the intent of connecting it to your local area network or the Internet.

Internet Connection

Desktop Hosting permits partners who have access to your machine to pull authorized information from it. On the Web, this access is supported by TCP/IP protocol (often shortened to IP, where both letters are pronounced). In this protocol, every communicating device has a numerical address. It is similar to a phone number for your computer, only there are four sets of numbers separated by dots (example: 204.188.26.66). This address is typically translated into a name to make it easier for people to remember (example: www.billyjames.com). This conversion is managed by DNS lookup tables, which are similar to automated yellow pages. The address translation follows these steps:

1. Enter a Web page address into a Web browser.
2. The browser sends a lookup request to the DNS server; it responds with the corresponding numerical address (phone number) with a path of connected servers to that IP address.
3. The browser requests Web pages from the translated IP address on that path.

You can find the IP address assigned to your desktop as follows:

Windows: Startup >> Control Panel >> Network >> TCP/IP Protocol. An alternative is to go to Startup >> Run, type in winipcfg and hit the Enter key.

Mac: AppleMenu >> Control Panel >> TCP/IP

This address may be fixed or it may vary depending on the design of your network. If you have questions about the nature of your setup, contact your network administrator or the provider of your Internet access (ISP or phone company). Remember that for a machine to be consistently available, you need a fixed IP address.

Although a fixed IP address on a network is necessary for others to consistently find your desktop-hosted site, it is possible to build and test your efforts without being connected to a network.

Local Setup: Working without an Internet Connection

A standard name (localhost) for a local Web host (a Web service running on your local desktop) was established to test Web servers. It allows the server and browser to operate on the same machine, simulating a network connection between the two. This is very useful when developing your site or when you are demonstrating hosting technology without access to the Web.

The conventional IP address to enter into the Web browser is

```
http://127.0.0.1
```

or simply the word

```
http://localhost
```

This address is a standard convention that tells the browser to query the local machine for Web services. It has nothing to do with the actual TCP/IP address of the computer.

NOTE

The default port is 80. If you have another Web server running on that port, you will need to either turn the other Web server off or change the port used by WebClerk in Web Prefs window.

NOTE

This address will work unless your network is set up with a proxy server that grabs the message from the browser and prevents the local server from responding. The proxy server can be instructed to allow you to use this address, or you can use the actual dotted IP address for your machine.

World Wide Web Setup Internet

Contact your Internet service provider to obtain a connection to a fixed TCP/IP address. If your provider will not supply you a fixed IP address, change vendors. You could not operate your company if your telephone numbers change every day; you cannot provide unattended communications without a fixed number for your Web server.

Your connection to the Web must be bidirectional; this is best done with a digital connection to the Web. It can be done with an analog connection, but the connection delay of analog is onerous. If only analog connections are available, it is best to "nail up" the connection—keep the line connected even when there is no traffic.

It is a good idea to map your dotted address to a real domain name using DNS so that it is easier for people to remember your site. Another benefit of this mapping is that if you move your site to a different machine with a different IP address, you need only send an update instruction to the DNS server to direct requests to the new dotted address.

Install WebClerk Application

Installation of WebClerk is quite straightforward. Because there are about 150 training movies on the CD that you are likely to need many times in the future, the CD does not launch an Auto-Installation session for installing WebClerk. Therefore, you will install it by doing the following:

1. Insert the WebClerk CD into your CD ROM drive.
2. Go to the CD ROM drive in your computer.
3. Double-click on the CD icon or open the CD.
4. Double-click on the installers folder.
5. Double-click on the desired installer folder depending on whether your computer is a PC or Mac.
6. Double-click on the WebClerk_Installer.exe to install it on your computer. Follow the installer instructions. It is generally best to install the WebClerk application in a root directory (avoid burying the folder inside other folders).

NOTE

If you have downloaded the appropriate self-extracting file (for Windows or Mac) from the Webclerk site (www.WebClerk.com), just double-click on the .exe, and it will install to a directory that you specify.

Key Folders and Documents

It is important to understand where things are stored on your hard drive. You will need to access various Web pages and graphics in editing applications.

Application

The folder in which WebClerk is launched sets the path for all other key folders. It is installed in a folder called WebClerk. A recommended path to this folder is:

PC	C:\WebClerk\WebClerk9_5.exe
Mac	HardDrive:WebClerk:WebClerk 9.5:

Figure 8.6 shows a list of files typical to the top-level WebClerk folder on a PC.

Web Site

The jitWeb folder contains all the pages that are capable of being served to the Web. The path to this folder is controlled relative to the application folder. Assuming WebClerk was installed as described above, the path would be:

PC	C:\WebClerk\jitWeb\
Mac	HardDrive:WebClerk:jitWeb:

You can customize the pages in this folder with any standard text or HTML editor. Care should be taken with some advanced HTML editors. They sometimes overhelp and wreck the database tags on the Web pages. They generally have a setting that prevents this from occurring.

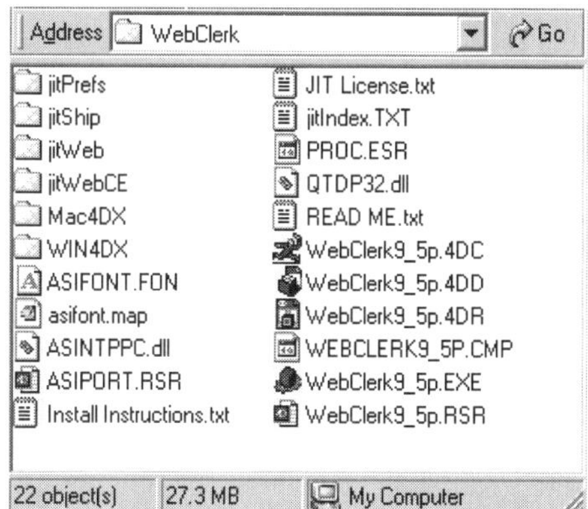

Figure 8.6 Typical WebClerk folder and contents.

Graphics, Movies, Documents, PDFs

Graphics and files to be served to the Web are generally stored in the images folder inside the jitWeb folder:

PC	C:\WebClerk\jitWeb\images\
Mac	HardDrive:WebClerk:jitWeb:images:

Set the graphics in the WebClerk Flow window by clicking on the Set Graphics button. Loading graphics through the WebClerk application may require QuickTime (free from www.apple.com) to be installed.

You may want to have some graphics customized for your site. Although this is not necessary, it will make more sense to you if the graphic logos are ready *before* configuring WebClerk.

TYPICAL GRAPHICS FILENAME	APPROXIMATE SIZE (PIXELS)
Logo_Main.gif	94 high × 406 wide
Logo_Nav.gif	32 high × 82 wide
Logo_Splash.gif	300 high × 300 wide

A good Web page developer will be able to customize the look and feel to whatever extent you wish to pay for. So start with these graphics guidelines, and experiment from there after you get a feel for how WebClerk works and how the HTML files are edited.

Launch WebClerk

The WebClerk executable is in the WebClerk folder. The exact filename will change depending on the version number and platform. The typical paths are listed under Application.

1. Double-click on the WebClerk application to launch it. A window will open asking for your username and password.
2. Click on the second user Click_Here_Then_Click_OK. This user's name is the same as the instruction. After selecting Click_Here_Then_Click_OK, click on the OK button in the lower right of the window. The demo database will open in the application unless you change the data set to be used.

Initial View of WebClerk

The demo data set for WebClerk has an opening default value of Learning Mode set to True. In this mode, four windows will open when you launch the application. Depending on the screen size, they will open either on top of each other or adjacent to each other (information on managing this feature can be found in TechNotes, keyword default). Those four windows are:

WebClerk Flow. Lists major features for setting up and running WebClerk. This window is discussed in detail later.

TechNotes. Contains searchable help, training movies, and technical notes. This window is explained earlier in this chapter. It is very important for the documentation of WebClerk and is available to you to add your own documentation. Close this window by clicking on OK or X in the navigation pallet in the upper left of the window. Open this window again by going to the Depts menu and selecting TechNote Reference.

Main. Behind all other windows is the Main Process splash screen for CommerceExpert. This is the only window that opens when launching the program with Learning Mode turned off. Review the Review TechNotes with Subject Menu and review movies in TechNotes; Name equals List of Movies.

Process. This small window keeps track of all open windows in the program. Clicking on a process will bring the window for that process to the front. Some processes, such as http servers, do not have process windows.

NOTE

A window that does not open but is very useful to review is the CommerceExpert Flow window. Open this window from the Depts menu >> CommerceExpert Flow.

General Navigation in WebClerk

The TechNote named Getting Started summarizes the navigation and structure of WebClerk. TechNotes provide a great deal of additional support. It is recommended that you review those with Subject Startup and Name List of Movies, and TechNotes Subject Menu.

QuickSummary

Because some people will not read program documentation, QuickSummary is a very brief summary of navigation in WebClerk. Data is organized in tables such as [Customers], [Items], [Vendors], and so forth. Go to the Depts menu and then to CommerceExpert Flow for a flow chart and list of Tables.

Tables of data are typically managed in three layers with different types of layouts:

Splash screens are used to manage which table is to be viewed. There are splash screens for the Sales, Production, and Admin Departments. WebClerk Flow and CommerceExpert Flow windows are splash screen windows. Menus across the top of the screen access specific features and tables in the Department splash screens. Buttons on the screens manage access in the WebClerk Flow and CommerceExpert Flow screens.

Output Layouts displays a list of records in a table. From a list, access a single record by double-clicking on it. Close an Output Layout by clicking on the OK button in the lower right.

Input Layouts open a record in a table for data management and display lists of related records. Fields in these layouts support data entry. These layouts can have multiple pages. Navigate Input Layouts with the Navigation Pallet in the upper-left corner. Use X to exit the window without saving changes, OK to close window and save changes, and < or > to view previous and next record in the table; if a pop-up menu is present, change the page of the Input Layout.

WebClerk Flow Window

The WebClerk flow screen provides a graphical interface to the many functions and database tables needed to manage your unattended communication interface with customers (see Figure 8.7).

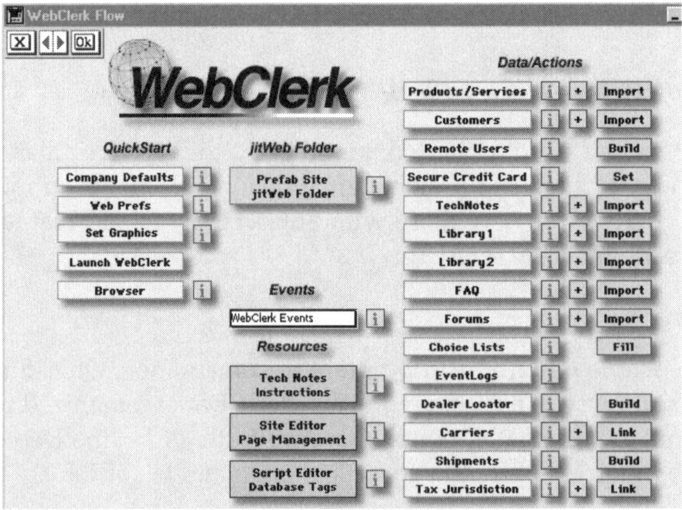

Figure 8.7 Management interface for WebClerk Flow.

Navigation and Action Buttons

The WebClerk Flow screen has graphics or buttons for navigation and feature management;

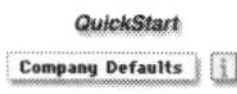

- Resource or Table buttons are the wide buttons listing specific features or database tables.

- Info (i) buttons call up the TechNotes relative to the specific Action or File button.

- The Plus (+) button adds a record to the adjacent table and opens it in a new process window for data entry.
- The Action button, such as Import, executes the typical first task required for a new data file.

QuickStart

QuickStart guides you through the key requirements to set up and run Web-Clerk:

Company Defaults. Opens the Defaults record to enter information about the company.

Web Prefs. Opens the WebClerk defaults.

Set Graphics. Allows you to use WebClerk to set basic graphics files into the prefabricated Web pages.

Launch WebClerk. Initiates the server capabilities of WebClerk.

Browser. Launches your browser to the server operating on your machine.

JitWeb Folder

jitWeb Folder is the prefabricated Web site, the templates through which Web-Clerk projects its server capabilities. Clicking on this button will open the jitWeb folder from your desktop. Note that sometimes the computer's operating system is not set up to accept this command, and you will have to navigate through your hard drive manually.

Events

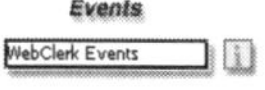

Events displays a list of TechNotes that have WebClerk Events as a keyword. If a specific TechNote is selected, it displays in the TechNote window. This is an expandable support area into which you may create additional TechNotes.

Resources

Resources opens editors that support the management of WebClerk and HTML pages. These are the detailed TechNotes.

Site Editor. This editor displays all the HTML pages in the jitWeb folder. See Chapter 6 and TechNotes for a review of this editor.

Script Editor. The Script Editor assists in a number of tasks:

- Writing executable scripts
- Drafting HTML pages
- Translating the structure of the database and recurring tools into an editor

Data/Actions

Data/Actions manages the database tables and their records. Clicking on a button will display the database records for the table that are published to the Web. Accessing all records is managed from the typical CommerceExpert splash screens.

Exercise in WebClerk Flow

Repeat the exercise listed in Table 3.1 of Chapter 3 of this book. In TechNotes there are additional exercises in those notes that have Subject Learning Exercises and Subject QuickSteps. Doing these exercises will help you understand WebClerk, the data structure, and Web site management. More exercises can be loaded from www.WebClerk.com.

Exercise in Customization

This section describes a bare-bones approach for customizing your site. It assumes:

- The network connections are available when you need them.
- Some graphics are ready for testing (you may also use the graphics provided on the CD, but they are obviously not customized to your business).
- You know how to use an external Web page editing program.

Initial Setup: QuickStart

1. Click on Company Defaults (QuickStart). The defaults record opens.
2. Enter your company name in the Company field. Edit other fields as desired.
3. Click on the OK button in the Navigation Pallet (upper left part of screen).

This will save the changes and return you to the WebClerk Flow window.

4. Click Web Prefs (QuickStart). This will open up the Web preferences.
5. Enter your values (does not affect your current named server, mail server, etc.)

Field	Example Field Values for : WineopsDomain	www.wineops.com
Mail Server:	If you do not have a mail server, leave this field blank or there will be long delays at order confirmation while mail is trying to be sent.	
Default eMail:	Example: mailto:service@ WebClerk.com	
Default jitWeb Folder:	C:\WEBCLERK\jitWeb\	

6. Click on the OK button in the right center of this dialog window to close it and save changes.
7. Click on Set Graphics. A window displays the current graphics in the WebClerk Flow. Create Web graphics to match these approximate graphics. You can paste your graphics in these windows to save them to the Web. When finished (it is not required that you change the graphics), click on the Cancel or Set Graphics buttons in the upper left of the window.
8. Click on Launch WebClerk to launch the Web serving capability. Clear the alert message that tells you that WebClerk has launched.
9. Click on Browser in the WebClerk Flow window or go to your desktop and launch a browser. In the browser type http://127.0.0.1 or http://localhost and hit Enter or go. The index.html page in the jitWeb folder will display (see key folder information earlier in this chapter).
10. Go to the jitWeb folder (see typical locations in the installation instructions earlier in this chapter) and make changes to the desired pages. Specifically change the Co_About.html page to view changes. This page is displayed in the browser when you click on the About URL.
11. Go to the jitWeb folder, open the images folder, and look at the graphics stored there to see where they are displayed in browser.
12. Customize the pages and graphics as needed.

More Exercises

Go to www.WebClerk.com to find additional learning exercise, forums, and other support.

Summary

There are training and support options available for WebClerk and Desktop Hosting in general. Dynamic information will regularly be updated on the Web.

You now have a small background in WebClerk. This is a pretty comprehensive program. Sometimes comprehensive is synonymous with complex. I encourage you to use the forums at www.webclerk.com to make suggestions and share solutions with others. As advocated throughout the book: Take small bites. Try out portions of the program that look interesting to your business. Gain experience and then tailor tools and techniques to meet the requirements of your company. Focus on increasing profitable sales, where profit is the difference between the value that customers pay for and the cost to compete.

Desktop Hosting is waiting to be leveraged to your advantage, putting the point of communications at the point of action. It increases the power of unattended communications and exercises the aspect of leadership that communicates to your trading partners the value of their relationship with your company.

Good luck in building these tools and techniques to your advantage.

Glossary of Terms and Products

B2B Business-to-business

B2C Business-to-consumer

Common-Data Rentable data set of current inventory information among businesses in a vertical market segment.

Common-Language The combination of Common-Data and Common-Tools.

Common-Tools The suite of JITCorp software components that comprises the e-commerce product:

WebClerk Desktop Hosting/Web serving software

CommerceExpert B2B enterprise software

RetailClerk Point-of-sale software

CRM Customer Relationship Management

DNS Domain Name Services

EDI Electronic Data Interchange

ERP Enterprise Resource Planning

ESO Enterprise Sales and Operations

HTML HyperText Markup Language. The underlying formatted file that makes up a Web page.

JITCorp James Integrated Technologies Corporation

MIME Multipurpose Internet Mail Extensions. A communications protocol that permits transmission of data in many formats, such as binary, audio, or video files.

OEMs Original Equipment Manufacturers

PDA Personal Digital Assistant, typically known as a palm or handheld device.

PDF Portable Document Format from Adobe Systems, Inc. (www.adobe.com)

SKU Stock Keeping Unit. Item numbers unique to each product and size.

SSL Secure Sockets Layer. This protocol was developed by Netscape for securely transmitting documents via the Internet. SSL works by using a public key to encrypt data that is transferred over the network connection. Web browsers and Web sites use the protocol to transmit private user information, such as credit card numbers. Note: By convention, Web addresses that require an SSL connection start with https: (instead of http:).

Sneaker net A manual data transport mechanism using people (sometimes wearing athletic shoes) carrying floppy disks from one computer to another.

SupplyChainSuite The entire collection of data and tools that permit seamless transactions among a fragmented industry.

TCP/IP Transmission Control Protocol/Internet Protocol, the suite of communications protocols used to connect hosts on the Internet. TCP/IP uses several protocols, the two main ones being TCP and IP. TCP/IP is built into the UNIX operating system and is used by the Internet, making it the de facto standard for transmitting data over networks. Even network operating systems that have their own protocols, such as Netware, also support TCP/IP.

10BaseT or **10Base-T** One of several adaptations of the Ethernet (IEEE 802.3) standard for Local Area Networks (LANs). The 10Base-T standard (also called Twisted Pair Ethernet) uses a twisted-pair cable with maximum lengths of 100 meters. The cable is thinner, cheaper, and more flexible than the coaxial cable used for the 10Base-2 or 10Base-5 standards.

UPC Universal Product Code (bar codes).

URL Universal Resource Locator. A URL is the global address of documents and other electronic resources on the Web. The first part of the address indicates what protocol to use, and the second part specifies the domain name or IP address where the resource is located. For example, the two URLs below point to two different files at the domain webclerk.com. The first specifies a Web page that should be pulled down using the http protocol; the second specifies an executable file that should be downloaded using the ftp protocol:

http://www.webclerk.com/index.html

ftp://www.webclerk.com/program1.exe

VPN Virtual Private Network. Public networks are used to connect computers or network devices, but the data transmitted across that public network is encrypted at both ends. This effectively creates a private network on a public network such as the Internet.

WineOps Wine Operations, Inc.

XML eXtensible Markup Language

What's on the CD-ROM

This appendix provides you with information on the contents of the CD that accompanies this book. For the latest and greatest information, please refer to the text files located at the root of the CD-ROM. The text files are:

1_JIT License.txt This is the license to use WebClerk/CommerceExpert, included on the CD-ROM. The software is fully functional with *no* time limits. Registration is not required, but it is recommended that you register your license at www.WebClerk.com.

2_READ_ME.txt This document provides important startup notes and known bug lists.

3_READ_Copyright.txt This document contains the formal copyright statement.

4_Tech_Support.txt This document contains the URL for technical support, plus details for contacting Wiley regarding technical problems with the CD-ROM.

System Requirements

Make sure that your computer meets the minimum system requirements listed in this section. If your computer doesn't match up to most of these requirements, you may have a problem using the contents of the CD.

For Windows 9*x*, Windows 2000, Windows NT4 (with SP 4 or later), Windows Me, or Windows XP:

- PC with a Pentium processor running at 200 Mhz or faster.
- At least 128 MB of total RAM installed on your computer; for best performance, we recommend at least 256 MB.
- A CD-ROM drive.
- A hard drive with at least 90 megabytes of free space.
- For the single-user version of the program that is distributed on the CD, a network connection is not necessary for it to function. However, if you need to visit the supporting Web sites for further information, appropriate access to the Internet is presumed.

For Macintosh:

- Mac OS computer with a PowerPC or faster processor running OS 8.6 or later.
- At least 128 MB of total RAM installed on your computer; for best performance, we recommend at least 256 MB.
- A CD-ROM drive.
- A hard drive with at least 90 megabytes of free space.
- For the single-user version of the program that is distributed on the CD, a network connection is not necessary for it to function. However, if you need to visit the supporting Web sites for further information, appropriate access to the Internet is presumed.

Installing Software from this CD

To install the items from the CD to your hard drive, you will need at least 90 MB of free disk space. Then follow these steps:

1. Insert the CD into your computer's CD-ROM drive. Because the CD may be used many times in the future to access the instructional movies, the autorun feature has been disabled for this CD.

2. Win: From the desktop or from Windows Explorer, double click on "My Computer" or whatever name you have renamed your computer to.

   Mac: Double-click on the icon for the CD after it appears on the desktop.
3. Double-click on your CD drive to open it.
4. Double-click on the Install_Win to view the correct installer. There is only one installer in each folder.
5. Double-click on the installer. Follow the installation instructions, selecting an appropriate Destination Directory of your choice. It will install into a directory named WebClerk (and other files under that) under your specified Destination Directory.
6. Go the directory where the WebClerk application is stored. Double-click on the WebClerk program icon to launch it.
7. A Password Dialog will open. Click on the second name on the list (this is the default administrative user)

   ```
   "Click_Here_Then_Click_OK"
   ```

   to select the user. Then click the OK button.

   The demo data file will open by default. This data file is named similar to the name of the WebClerk application. In this case, the data file name is: WebClerk950p.4DD
8. In the demo data, the program will open to the Tech Notes screen, with Getting Started instructions displayed. Please read these.

   If you drag through the list in the upper right side and click the adjacent Print button, the selected Notes will print.
9. After you have completed the training exercises in the demo data, you will want to create your own data file and change the name of this demo data so it does not automatically open every time you start the WebClerk application. See the built-in Tech Note for how this is done.

What's on the CD

The following sections provide a summary of the software and other materials you'll find on the CD.

Author-Created Materials

The default sample dataset, examples, and movies are on the CD.

- The sample datasets are embedded during the software program installation, and are not discernible directly on the CD.

- Examples_JITCorp contains examples of applying Desktop Hosting principles to certain vertical industries.
- IntelligentTransportation contains a description of applying Desktop Hosting principles to the subject of personal transportation.
- Movies contains all the Help and Training movies that are called from within the built-in Tech Notes. If you have a movie viewer (such as QuickTime) running independently from the program, the MOV files may be viewed individually, directly from the CD.

Applications

The following applications are on the CD:

CommerceExpert / WebClerk, from James Integrated Technologies, Corp.

The author provides a full, free single-user version of the program. Specific licensing details are in the file the license file (1_JIT License.txt) located at the root of the CD-ROM. For additional information, see www.webclerk.com

Shareware programs are fully functional, trial versions of copyrighted programs. If you like particular programs, register with their authors for a nominal fee and receive licenses, enhanced versions, and technical support. *Freeware programs* are copyrighted games, applications, and utilities that are free for personal use. Unlike shareware, these programs do not require a fee or provide technical support. *GNU software* is governed by its own license, which is included inside the folder of the GNU product. See the GNU license for more details.

Trial, demo, or evaluation versions are usually limited either by time or functionality (such as being unable to save projects). Some trial versions are very sensitive to system date changes. If you alter your computer's date, the programs will "time out" and will no longer be functional.

Troubleshooting

If you have difficulty installing or using any of the materials on the companion CD, try the following solutions:

Turn off any anti-virus software that you may have running. Installers sometimes mimic virus activity and can make your computer incorrectly believe that it is being infected by a virus. (Be sure to turn the anti-virus software back on later.)

Close all running programs. The more programs you're running, the less memory is available to other programs. Installers also typically update files and programs; if you keep other programs running, installation may not work properly.

Reference the ReadMe. Please refer to the ReadMe file (2_READ_ME.txt) located at the root of the CD-ROM for the latest product information at the time of publication.

If you still have trouble with the CD, please call the Wiley Customer Care phone number: (800) 762-2974. Outside the United States, call 1 (317) 572-3994. Wiley will provide technical support only for installation and other general quality control items; for technical support on the applications themselves, consult the program's vendor or author.

INDEX

P

Q

R

CUSTOMER NOTE: IF THIS BOOK IS ACCOMPANIED BY SOFTWARE, PLEASE READ THE FOLLOWING BEFORE OPENING THE PACKAGE.

This software contains files to help you utilize the models described in the accompanying book. By opening the package, you are agreeing to be bound by the following agreement:

This software product is sold as is without warranty of any kind, either express or implied, including but not limited to the implied warranty of merchantability and fitness for a particular purpose. Neither Wiley nor its dealers or distributors assumes any liability for any alleged or actual damages arising from the use of or the inability to use this software. (Some states do not allow the exclusion of implied warranties, so the exclusion may not apply to you.)